JESUS AND MONEY

Dr. Paul Cannings

Lighting Source Inc. | *La Vergne Tennessee*

Please send your comments and requests for information to the address below:

Power Walk Ministries
7350 West T.C. Jester Blvd.
Houston, TX 77088
Telephone (281) 260-7402
www.lwfchurch.net

For more information concerning other products we offer including:

"Biblical Answers For the 21st Century Church"
ISBN 978-0-9779840-3-6
"Keeping Love Alive Series" for strengthening marriages or the "Leadership Training Series" for training leaders
Visit our website at **www.lwfchurch.net/**

For more information about speaking engagements, please contact Power Walk Ministries at (281) 260-7402.

Contents

Preface

This book is written in a Christian environment that addresses this issue from two differing perspectives. Each perspective is passionately debated with supporting evidence. I am by no means seeking to solve the issue of prosperity theology or to attack or support those who propagate this doctrine. This would lead to a doctrinal dissertation on the issue. This is not the purpose that I have in mind.

This book views God as seriously concerned about our well being, but also truly committed to us not being overcome by the world. Whether anyone believes in prosperity and opposes it, each person would agree they need God's provision to take care of their families. No one can go to the grocery store and announce that they love Jesus and are a faithful member in good standing of the neighborhood church and expect the owner to give them the groceries free of charge.

As much as we may all like to see that, it is not a daily reality. We need God's resources to properly manage our homes, send our children to college, settle into a not so dangerous community, deal with health issues, and prepare for all the changes of growing older. Does God provide a prescription that blesses us?

i

I strongly believe that the Bible is our guide that must direct our conclusions. The Bible must not become an agent that serves as a footnote to what we believe. The Bible must be the road map that directs the way to a destination that blesses our lives and our families. When various passages are addressed, the rules of exegesis must determine our Biblical conclusions. Without this, earthly wisdom directs our lives, not the Holy Spirit the illuminator of God's Word who guides us into truth (John 16:13).

It is this process that allowed the New Testament to resolve issues, not create more confusion. The churches were not confused after a letter was written by the apostles. They were healed from controversy and empowered to be productive for the glory of God and their blessing.

This book is dedicated to all those who sincerely love God and truly want to walk in His ways but can't seem to find ways to become more productive with the resources God has provided. It seeks to increase their faith, make firm their hope and deepen their resolve that God cares about their daily struggle to provide for their families and truly wants to bless each and everyday for His glory and honor.

Acknowledgements

I would like to first thank my wife, Everette, for her consistent support. She has been my friend, partner, and my wife for 27 years. Anyone that can do this for this long must truly love me. I thank God for His goodness.

I would also like to thank my children, Paul Jr., Pierre and Pierre's wife, Monica, for their encouragement and steadfast love for their father, friend and spiritual leader.

I also would like to thank the leaders and members of Living Word Fellowship Church for the confidence they show in the leadership God has blessed me to provide. Their willingness to trust that God is at work in me to do a good work for His glory and honor.

I also thank my staff for their hard work and support. I would like to thank the Power Walk board for their steadfast support. I would like to also thank Mayphous Collins for his diligent work in preparing this book for publication.

Without these supporters and the sacrifices they have so willingly made, there is no way the Living Word Fellowship Church and Power Walk Ministries would be where it is today. To all, I sincerely thank you.

C H A P T E R **1**

Rags to Riches

"And without faith it is impossible to please God, because anyone who comes to <u>Him must believe that He exists and that He rewards those who earnestly seek Him."</u> (Hebrews 11:6-7; NIV). This verse was true when the Bible was written, and it is still true today. When we exercise faith in God, we are sure about what we hope for and certain of what we do not see.

Our faith is not tested when life is functioning according to our plans. Our faith is tested when circumstances are difficult and our experiences are overwhelming. Circumstances can either deepen our commitment to God, or if we are not careful, those same circumstances can cause us to abandon God. Faith is the element which allows us to earnestly seek Him. As a result, by having faith in God, we place ourselves in a position to receive the reward that He already has for us.

Our prosperity is never dependent on our circumstances or what someone is doing to us. Our prosperity is dependent on what God can do for us based on our faithfulness to Him. Some believers think that if they gamble and hit the jackpot then God has blessed them. Some believers hang out at night clubs with friends so that they can remain good friends with the people on the job. Some believers cheat and stab others in the back to get a raise or promotion. However, one cannot indulge in unrighteousness and still expect to be blessed by God (Prov. 28:20).

We must still hold to His truth and obey Him. We cannot turn from God even if the rags are getting to us and poverty is hurting us. We must still be about our Master's business. We cannot be dishonest in our dealings and then expect God to bless us. Being committed to living a Christian life leads to powerful results. *"Wealth obtained by fraud dwindles, but the one who gathers by labor increases it."* (Proverbs 13:11; NASU)

In His word, God shows us individuals whose faithfulness allowed them to be promoted from a level of being in rags, to the status of gaining riches. Genesis 37-50, tells the rags to riches story of Joseph, the son of Jacob. Jacob had 12 sons, but Joseph was his favorite. This favoritism caused his brothers to dislike him. In the story, Joseph had a dream that his brothers were bowing down to him. This dream caused his brothers to dislike him even more and so Joseph's brothers began to plot against him.

Their plot led them to selling him to the Ishmaelites. Joseph was later sold to Potiphar in Egypt. While in Egypt, Joseph's master, Potiphar, noticed that the Lord was with Joseph and brought him success in whatever he did. Since the Lord was with Joseph, his master placed him in charge of his household and entrusted all his possessions to Joseph. *"From the moment that he put him in charge of his household and all his possessions, the Lord blessed the Egyptian's house for Joseph's sake"* (Genesis 39:5). Later, while in Potiphar's house, Joseph was thrown in prison after false accusations from Potiphar's wife. She accused him of trying to sleep with her.

However, even in prison, the Lord was with Joseph and gave him success in everything (Genesis 39:23). As the story continues, Pharoah, the king of Egypt, had mysterious dreams and needed an interpreter. At that time, Joseph was summoned, because he was the only person who had the ability to interpret the dream. When the king summoned Joseph to interpret the dream, Joseph recognized that it was not his ability that allowed him to interpret dreams. Joseph told Pharoah, *"It is not I, but God, who will give Pharoah the right answer." (Genesis 41:16)*

Joseph, through God's power, interpreted Pharoah's dream as a vision that there would be seven years of abundance in Egypt, followed by seven years of famine. Joseph was then placed in charge of food management in Egypt. When the famine came, the whole world came to Egypt to buy food from Joseph. Joseph's brothers now had to come to him for food. Joseph forgave his brothers for selling him to the Ishamaelites, because he realized that his journey was all a part of God's plans for his life. Joseph acknowledges God's omniscience when he tells his brothers, *"As for you, you meant evil against me, [but] God meant it for good in order to bring about this present result, to preserve many people alive."* (Genesis 50:20)

The success we gain is not only acquired due to positive circumstances, but sometimes God uses negative situations to bless His people. Joseph remained focused on God in the midst of the difficulty he experienced. Joseph understood that *"... all things work together for good to those who love God, to those who are called according to his purposes."* (Romans 8:28) Joseph did not take credit for his success. Joseph recognized that it was God who deserved the glory for his success. Joseph's success was a result of his faithfulness to God.

In the book of Daniel, the Bible tells us of yet another individual who was promoted from rags to riches. In 722 BC, the people of Judah watched the Northern kingdom Israel be destroyed due to their unwillingness to listen to God. God provided preachers like Isaiah (a prophet who was the most quoted by Jesus) and Jeremiah, but the people of Judah refused to listen. The Babylonians came in and destroyed the city just as Jeremiah told them they would.

After their homes and their city were destroyed, one particular young teenage boy, who came from a royal lineage, was among those who walked nine hundred miles to a different county, possibly stepping over bodies and other wreckage; all because Israel refused to listen to God. While on this journey, he had to eat whatever he was given and sleep wherever they told him to sleep. This young man, by the name of Daniel, was ripped from his family and arrived in Babylon in rags. He was then subjected to taking orders from brutal King Nebuchadnezzar.

This king was demanding that Daniel learn his language, eat his food, worship his god and serve him. Although Daniel was in a difficult situation, he never complained. Daniel stayed focused on obeying God. There were other youth who came along with Daniel (Daniel 1:10, 13). Unlike Daniel, those young people simply adapted to their circumstances, rather than remaining committed to God. Daniel did not join in with the other youth, because it was the popular thing to do.

Daniel remained committed to God despite the fact that he had to eat vegetables and water for more than three years. *"But Daniel <u>made up his mind</u> that he would not defile himself with the kings' choice food or with the wine which he drank; so he sought permission from the commander of the officials that he might not defile himself."* (Daniel 1:8) The other youth lived out the course of their lives, but they never became as powerful or wealthy as Daniel.

Daniel teaches us that living a godly life must be our first priority. Daniel took the opportunity that God gave to him and worked hard to please God in all that he did. Daniel did not complain, despite the difficult circumstances that he was enduring. He took advantage of the opportunity that God provided him. After all, not every captive was allowed to work for the king. There were many captives who could have worked in more difficult situations. Daniel saw his opportunity as a blessing. There were other wise men that were of greater stature than him who could have had his position. Daniel started at the bottom of the ladder and had to learn everything from the beginning, including a new language.

Daniel took the schooling that he was given, worked hard for three years, and he gave his best. He did this as a service to God. Some of us, on the other hand, are not blessed because we are so busy complaining, that we allow opportunities to pass us by. God has placed us on jobs that sometimes provide an education in a particular skill or may pay for classes at a local college. God sometimes gives us a chance to move up the ladder, and we spend more time complaining about where we are, than acknowledging where He can take us. The scripture teaches that the person who is faithful over a few things, God blesses them with more (Matthew 25:21). *Commit your works to the LORD and your plans will be established* (Proverbs 16:3; NASU). *"In all labor there is profit, but mere talk leads only to proverty.* (Proverbs 14:23; NASU).

We should be grateful for the jobs that God blesses us with. In addition to being grateful for our jobs, we must also follow the rules and regulations that the job outlines to us. God's blessings are not provided when believers function with disrespect to their company policies. Some Christians arrive to work late at 8:30 a.m. when they were supposed to be there at 8 o'clock. We must remember that our service is not to men, but to God, because it is God who blesses us. Believers are rewarded when we take the work that He has provided and we apply ourselves to the task faithfully. *"Poor is he who works with a negligent hand, but the hand of the diligent makes rich."* (Proverbs 10:4; NASU)

There are some people who act as if their gifts come from their education, or from their ability to survive, or from their likeability, or from being in the right place at the right time. However, we need to remember that ALL good things were bestowed by God. God is the one who blessed us so that we may even have a job. So in our daily service on our jobs, we should remember the verse which states, *Whatever you do, do your work heartily, as for the Lord rather than for men, knowing that from the Lord you will receive the reward of the inheritance. It is the Lord Christ whom you serve."* (Colossians 3:22-24; NASU) We should perform our labor for the glory of God.

Sometimes, it is difficult to understand why the wicked are allowed to prosper. Despite all the wickedness that surrounded Daniel, he did not become upset over the fact that the wicked men seemed to prosper. God allowed the wicked to prosper, but if they continued in their sinful ways, He was also the one who brought them down. Strangely, God prospers the wicked sometimes so that we can prosper. *"A good man leaves an inheritance to his children's children, and the wealth of the sinner is stored up for the righteous."* (Proverbs 13:22)

If Nebuchadnezzar was not a powerful and mighty king when the Jews came to Babylon, they would not have been as prosperous as they were. If the unsaved were not prosperous, then there may be a lot less businesses. When God decided to humble King Nebuchadnezzar, he was not allowed back to his kingdom until the Lord said so. Daniel advised the brutal king to break away from his sins, but he refused. God had blessed King Nebuchadnezzar, but he became arrogant and indignant about what God had done for him. As a result, God stripped him of his power. The king professed that Daniel was a righteous man and that God lived in him, yet he himself refused to live righteous. There was no one who would go against the brutal king.

As Daniel and others were suffering, the king was prospering. Did this deter Daniel from serving his God and being faithful? Absolutely not. In fact, this gave Daniel an opportunity to be blessed. Daniel at one point became wealthier than the king. At one point, the king was eating grass for seven years while Daniel was in charge of the palace. *"The wages of the righteous is life, the income of the wicked, punishment."* (Proverbs 10:16; NASU)

Daniel's incredible faith led an entire nation to worship God. When jealous 'wise men' sought to destroy Daniel, God gave him favor with the king and protected him in the lion's den. God destroyed his accusers and gave Daniel even greater blessings while turning the entire nation to worship the true Lord God (Daniel chapter 6). It is better to be promoted by God, because whoever is established by God cannot be moved. *"A man will not be established by wickedness, but the root of the righteous will not be moved."* (Proverbs 12:3; NASU)

Daniel also showed us that we must not worship idol gods. When King Nebuchadnezzar decided that he was going to build a grand image, he told everyone to worship this image. Daniel said he was not going to do it, despite the fact that he was dealing with a brutal king. He worked for the king, but he was not going to compromise his faith. Some of us make our jobs our god, and we have compromised our worship to God over a job because that job becomes our salvation. The Bible stated to serve the Lord, give Him time and let Him become the priority. *"Great wealth is in the house of the righteous, but trouble is in the income of the wicked." (Prov 15:6; NASU)*

For some of us, the idol god is television. We worship the television on Saturday night and come to church on Sunday and rush out to watch the tube again.

For some of us, the idol god is money. We would compromise our religion for money. While going to eat in a restaurant in Freeport, Bahamas, I had to pass through a casino. Before reaching the restaurant, I saw a lady with tubes coming from an oxygen tank all the way to her nostrils and she was busy gambling. She was barely breathing oxygen by the grace of God and she was still gambling looking for the big jackpot.

I was telling a fellow preacher who accompanied me that she should not even have been there. He then informed me that there have been people who have died there right before their gods. There are people doing this all the time, because money is their god. We are so busy that we do not even know why we are busy. When it is time to serve the Lord with commitment, dedication and drive, we have no energy left. In order for God to bless us, we must put him first. *"But seek for His kingdom, and these things shall be added to you. Do not be afraid, little flock, you're your Father has chosen gladly to give you the kingdom."* (Luke 12:31-32)

The success that we experience does not mean that difficulties are not going to occur. Sometimes believers function as if because we are doing what God has called us to do, everything will go better. If we experience difficult job situations, then we may think that our jobs are not in the will of God and maybe we are in the wrong place. Daniel could have thought this, because after he was trained, the king had a dream. King Nebuchadnezzar stated that he was not going to tell the conjurers the dream because they were going to make something up. He told them to tell him what the dream was and then tell him the interpretation. Daniel now had problems on his job, because the king was going to try and kill all the magicians, conjurers and sorcerers in Babylonian, including Daniel and his friends (Daniel 2:18). The magicians, conjurers and sorcerers said that there was no way for them to know what the king was thinking (Daniel 2:10).

In this intense struggle, God was blessing Daniel because none of the king's experienced "wise men" could respond to the king. Instead of Daniel running away in fear to seek a place to hide, Daniel went to his friends and sought God (Daniel 2:17-18). Even though Daniel had received special insight into the training provided by the king (Daniel 1:17), it was not until Daniel sought God that he received special insight from God into the king's dream. *"Then the mystery was revealed in Daniel in the night vision. Then Daniel blessed the God of heaven. Daniel answered and said, `Let the name of God be blessed forever and* *ever, for wisdom and power belong to Him."* (Daniel 1:19)

Daniel developed a song of praise to God `from whom all blessings flow.' If Daniel had not decided to walk with God by submitting to his laws, not only would the magicians, conjurers and sorcerers have lost their lives, but Daniel and his friends would have died after enjoying the best of the best in the king's palace (Proverbs 28:20). God's compassion saved not just Daniel and his friends, but also all the other `wise men.' This established Daniel from the bottom of seniority list to the top (Daniel 2:48-49).

Could you imagine this powerful king, in the most powerful nation of the known world, during that period of history, bowing to Daniel? The king did not just bow to Daniel, but the Bible vividly states that the king `fell on his face and did homage to Daniel and gave order to present to him an offering and fragrant incense.'* (Daniel 2:46) In Daniel 2:8, we see that Daniel received his first success, not because he tried to cheat or get over on someone or work overtime on the job, but because he simply served the Lord. He faithfully served and in the midst of adversity he prayed.

In Daniel 2:46, it tells us that the king promoted Daniel and gave him great gifts and made him ruler over the whole providence of Babylon. Daniel was set up and he was "the man." This promotion did not just elevate Daniel it promoted God in the eyes of Nebuchadnezzar. He said *"surely your God is a God of gods and a Lord of kings and a revealer of mysteries, since you have been able to reveal this mystery."* (Daniel 2:47) Daniel's enemy, that once destroyed his people and his country, now bow to him (Daniel 2:26).

In Daniel 2:49, it states that Daniel went back to his prayer partners and promoted them also. Daniel understood who blessed and protected him and who cared for him. Daniel set his friends up by making them rulers over the administration of Babylon. Daniel demonstrated that he was a man of integrity. In the story Daniel constantly mentions the name of God, and sought to let King Nebuchadnezzar know who has the power to interpret dreams. King Nebuchadnezzar could only say *"Surely your God is a God of gods and a Lord of kings and a revealer of mysteries since you have been able to reveal this."* (Daniel 2:47) This victory, provided by the power of God, promoted Daniel and made him prosper. As a result, Daniel moves from rags to riches.

The success we experience does not always rely on an accumulation of positive circumstances. God sometimes uses negative situations to bless His people (Romans 8:28; 2 Corinthians 12:7-10). *"He humbled you and let you be hungry, and fed you with manna which you did not know, nor did your fathers know, that he might make you understand that man does not live by bread alone, but man lives by everything that proceeds out of the mouth of the Lord. Your clothing did not wear out on you, nor did your foot swell these forty years. Thus you are to know I your heart that the Lord your God was disciplining you just as a man disciplines his son. Therefore, you shall keep commandment of the Lord your God, to walk in His ways and to fear Him."* (Deut. 8:3-6; NASU) Daniel remained focused on God in the midst of the difficulty he experienced. Daniel's success was a result of his committed life to God, his prayer life and his trust in God.

God does not necessarily want every Christian to be rich (John 12:8), but He does not necessarily want every Christian to be poor either. The apostle Paul, after committing to follow Christ, (Acts 9) experienced tremendous difficulty and had to work harder than all the other apostles (1 Corinthians 15:10).

Paul would say, *"Not that I speak from want, for I have learned to be content in whatever circumstances I am. I know how to get along with humble means, and I also know how to live in prosperity; in any and every circumstance I have learned the secret of being filled and going hungry, both of having abundance and suffering need. I can do all things through Him who strengthens me."* (Philippians 4:11-13, NASU) Paul regularly told us not to complain about our circumstances and do not grumble against God, as the nation of Israel, and suffer (Philippians 2:14;

Colossians 3:13; 1 Corinthians 10:9-13). The Lord instructs us to have the same mindset as Paul. *"Rejoice always; pray without ceasing; in everything give thanks; for this is God's will for you in Christ Jesus. Do not quench the Spirit ..."* (1 Thessalonians 5:16-20, NASU)

No matter what we are going through, in order to move from rags to riches, we must let our lives be centered on serving the Lord and him only, no matter the circumstances. It may look like you are moving nowhere fast, but if believers remain faithful to the Lord and do not grow weary, we will be elevated. *"Let us not lose heart in doing good, for in due time we will reap if we do not grow weary."* (Galatians 6:9; NASU) *"The righteous is delivered from trouble, but the wicked takes his place."* (Proverbs 11:8; NASU)

You may get an education, or already have an education, but in order to have an inspired knowledge into all the information that is acquired, a believer must experience God's favor. So when ideas begin to pop up and these ideas produce productive results, it is because God, through the power of the Holy Spirit, blessed the process. *"Commit to the Lord whatever you do, and your plans will be blessed"* (Proverbs 16:3).

When God's hand is involved in anything, we can expect great results over time; His time. *"Unless the Lord builds the house, they labor in vain who build it; unless the Lord guards the city, the watch man keeps awake in vain. It is vain for you to rise up early, to retire late, to eat the bread of painful labors; for he gives to His beloved even in his sleep."* (Psalm 127:1-2; NASU)

"How blessed is everyone who fears the Lord, who walks in His ways, when you shall eat of the fruit of your hands you will be happy and it will be well with you." (Psalm 128:-2; NASU) It is not how many resources we may accumulate that determines success; it is how much faith we exercise. Our blessings from God depend on our faithfulness to the standards of God. *"It is the blessing of the* LORD *that makes rich, and He adds no sorrow to it."* (Proverbs 10:22; NASU)

C H A P T E R **2**

Overcoming Poverty

Poverty is all around us. It is not something that is just for a selected few, and it is not only in third world countries. The Bible told us that poverty and the poor are going to continually be among us. Jesus said this to Judas who acted as if he cared about the poor in John 12:8. Why does poverty take over? Why do some people prosper, while others continue in poverty?

The fact of the matter is, that if we do not have a mindset that is Biblically oriented, poverty can find us and consume us at any time. God is the one who has total control of our financial state and it is He who determines who sustains wealth. God has the last word about who is going to be rich and who will barely make it everyday.

We tend to think that, based on our education and experience; we can gain wealth and sustain our wealth by investing wisely. However, we must include God in our financial plans or it will be difficult for us to maintain the wealth gained from God's blessings. Many individuals feel secure because they have good jobs, at least three months worth of savings set aside, and all of their needs are met. However, if we do not have a strategy that is based on the principles outlined in God's Word, then we will not sustain prosperity and poverty will catch us like an armed bandit.

If we do not want to live in poverty, then we must not live like sluggards. God does not want us to live the lifestyle of a sluggard. In Proverbs 26:13-15, Solomon discusses the sluggard, when he says, *"There is a lion in the road! A lion is in the open square! As the door turns on its hinges, so does the sluggard on his bed. The sluggard buries his hand in the dish; He is weary of bringing it to his mouth again. The sluggard is wiser in his own eyes than seven men who can give a discreet answer."* (NASU) The sluggard is wise in his own eyes and never wants advice from anyone. Twenty years may go by, and sluggards may insist that they know what to do in order to reach their goals, but nothing has been done. *"The hand of the diligent will rule but the slack hand will be put to forced labor."* Proverbs 12:24

So who does God consider to be a sluggard? A sluggard is someone that has many dreams and desires, but does not want to put forth the efforts to fulfill those dreams and desires. If you desire to buy a house and you are not working towards your desire, then you are a sluggard. If you have a dream to be promoted or to make more money, and have not made one attempt towards that dream, then you are a sluggard. If you desire to get a Bachelors degree and you have done nothing toward gaining your education, then you are a sluggard. If you want to lose twenty pounds and you have not changed your eating habits or exercised, then you are a sluggard.

A sluggard is also someone who sees what needs to be done and does nothing about it. Sluggards like to procrastinate, and then they want to know why life is not getting any better. When you know what needs to be done on the job and you put it off until the last minute, then you are behaving like a sluggard. When the alarm clock goes off in the morning, and you repeatedly hit the snooze button again and again, then you are behaving like a sluggard.

I have a rule in my house, which says that my sons must get to work at least ten minutes early because the bosses are watching their clocks. My son was lying in bed and ran the risk of being late for work. He works for Living Word Christ Academy, which is a ministry of the church I pastor. My wife oversees our two pre-schools at the academy. So when my son said "Mama is my boss," I said "So what. If I have to wake you up the next day, you will lose your job.

There are two passages of scripture that shape the principles addressed in this chapter. Proverbs 6:6-11 states, *"Go to the ant, O sluggard, observe her ways and be wise, which, having no chief, officer or ruler, prepares her food in the summer and gathers her provision in the harvest. How long will you lie down, sluggard? When will you arise from your sleep? "A little sleep, a little slumber, a little folding of the hands to rest" — your poverty will come in like a vagabond and your need like an armed man."* (NASU)

This scripture is apparent to me when I work in my yard. There are times when the weeds in my yard annoy me, and I will go out and try to clear out the flower bed. While I am doing this, I run into a lot of different kinds of insects. One particular insect that has made an impression on me is the ant. Ants always seem so busy. They always have somewhere to go and something to do. They are always working diligently and they do not even have a boss. In fact, they have no leader; the queen is only there to produce more ants. The person who is a sluggard should learn from the ants. In fact, God shows us three valuable lessons from the lifestyle of an ant. These lessons will help us in our efforts to overcome poverty and sustain wealth.

The first lesson that we can learn from the ant is to prepare for a rainy day. We should prepare for incidentals or possible hardships that may occur in life. When rain falls on an ant mount, the ants survive, because when the rain falls they provide channels in their ant nest that will drain the rain. Ants have three levels in their nests. They have one level which is deep in the ground, which is where they store their food. The second level is for the ants that die. The third level is where the ants live. They have no one instructing them, but they go out and find food. The oldest ant will always go first and the ant with the heaviest burden will always get ahead of every other ant. They will pile food in their nest, and it does not matter which ant brought the food or which one gets food. They know how much to set aside for the winter based on how many ants are in the nest. They calculate it to the decimal point, so that when the winter comes they can live in their ant nest and never die of starvation.

Ants always prepare themselves for hardships that may occur. Unfortunately, many believers do not prepare themselves as well as ants. We have a bad habit of not saving. We often act as if a drought is never coming. In fact, most people are two checks away from poverty. Many people will get a raise and then buy a new car or a new house.

However, during our harvest, we must set aside money for a rainy day. We should not get a raise and immediately spend the money. The top priorities in our budgets should be first giving to God, depositing money into a saving account, and then paying our rent or mortgage and food. We should also set aside money for health, life and car insurances, and money for needed clothes. When we make wise decisions, God will guide us. "*In his heart a man plans his course, but the Lord determines his steps.*" (Proverbs 16:9)

The ant knows that there will not always be a time of harvest. The ant thinks, "let me preserve in the harvest because this is a blessed crop and I need to make sure that I have some resources set aside just in case a drought occurs." Proverbs 6:8 tells us that they gather for provision in the harvest.

Unfortunately, when life seems to be going well, some of us spend every bit of money we make. However, the Bible informs us that we will have trials (1 Peter 4:12) and that difficult days are ahead for the world as Christ prepares to return (Matthew 24). Many believers always have to have the newest, most expensive items, and as a result are constantly over-extended financially. God wants believers to change their lifestyles, because like the ant, we must preserve some of our harvest for difficult days.

The second lesson that we can learn from the ant is that we must decide to work without being told to work. As the ants work to prepare for a rainy day, they do this without any supervision. Like ants, we should work, simply because the work needs to be done. If someone has to make you get up to go to work, then you are not considering the ant. If someone has to make you clean the house when it is obviously dirty, then you are not considering the ant. A sluggard is someone that needs a supervisor. To avoid being like the sluggard, we must let our own desires and passions drive us to our dreams.

The third lesson that we can learn from the ant is that we must continue to work, despite adverse conditions. It does not matter how hot, dry, or how terrible the burning sun is, the ant continues to work. The ants do not let the weather conditions stop them from working. Like the ants, we cannot wait until circumstances are great before we move forward. If what we are trying to do is within God's desire for us, then He will guide our steps (Proverbs 16:9). A sluggard is waiting for conditions to be right. The ants do not wait, because they know what needs to be done, and what needs to happen.

Many believers spiritualize what needs to get done and as a result become sluggards in the Lord. Many believers will say, "Lord I am waiting on you to give me direction and tell me what to do." However, we are not waiting on the Lord. We just do not want to put forth the proper effort. We devise prayer meetings so that God can do what *we* need to do. Some people pray for God to help them find a job, but they do not spend every day looking for a job. Some people pray that their kids will do well in school, but they do not demand that their children turn off the television or stereo, get off the phone, and do their work.

We wait on the Lord to tell us what to do when He has already spoken from Genesis to Revelation. He said in His word, *"Ask and it will be given to you; seek and you will find; knock and the door will be opened to you. For everyone who asks receives; he who seeks finds; and to him who knocks, the door will be opened."* (Matthew 7:7-8) If we wait to hear from Him, then we must give our best efforts, and not expect our journey to always go smoothly.

When the children of Israel were doing well, they turned their backs on God. No matter how many prophets God sent to instruct them, they did not listen. However, when difficulties came and they were experiencing starvation, heavy taxation, and were being oppressed they expected God to deliver quickly. This is the type of behavior that sluggards practice.

Sluggards are people who want to party during the good times and not work during the bad times. They do not want to reap from their labor, they just want to reap. They do not want to work, but on payday they do not call in sick. The sluggard is happy about payday, but half the check is gone before they get home. The fact is, when things are going well, this is the time to pay off bills, because a time is going to come when you it may be difficult to pay all the bills.

In Proverbs 9:6, the sluggards are asked how long they are going to lie down? This question is asked because sluggards always do three things. Typically, sluggards lie down, go to sleep, and then they slumber. They do not just sleep, but they enjoy getting into deep sleep patterns. The hands they are supposed to put to work, they fold and rest them (Proverbs 9:10). This is not a good lifestyle.

Some people just love to sleep and they cannot wait until Saturday morning. My son brought a college friend home, and for the entire week he only slept and ate. I sat him down and told him that he was not going to make it in life like this and he did not listen. He was an awesome football player. He was picked up by an NFL team and whenever he felt like playing, he did extremely well in practice. After weeks of being in training camp, the coach told him that he could make any team in the NFL, but he was too lazy. He lost a $200,000 salary because he was too lazy.

The Bible says you need just a little sleep and a little slumber; not a whole lot. This means if you stay in the bed longer than you are supposed to, slumber, fold your hands not wanting to work, then your poverty will come in like a vagabond. Poverty will come and remove you from any sense of wealth.

In Matthew, we read of the servant who had one talent and he buried it. Christ called him a lazy and worthless servant when he said, *"you knew that I reap where I did not sow, and gather where I scattered no seed, then you ought to have put my money in the bank, and on my arrival I would have received my money back with interest."* (Matthew 25:26-27) The servant was so lazy he could not make it to the bank to invest the money. This is assuming that he even thought of taking it to the bank.

The owner took the one talent from this lazy servant and gave it to the person with five talents. This is why the rich get richer and the poor get poorer. We say that we are being exploited by those that are rich, and sometimes this is true, but it is also because we choose to live a lifestyle that is worthless. They choose to get up at six o'clock in the morning and go to the office to put in hard work. They choose to take risks, while we choose to slumber. Many people want to make excuses for not achieving success. However, we must remember that God is the one through whom all blessings flow. Therefore, we must focus on completing the tasks He demands from us.

We must also have a passion for what we would like to accomplish in our lives. *"Where there is no vision, the people are unrestrained, but happy is he who keeps the law."* (Proverbs 29:18; NASU) God has provided each of us with special abilities. We discover what those abilities are by exploring all of the options that school has to offer. This begins in elementary school and continues throughout our college years.

If a person finds that no matter how much time he or she invests in academics they do not grasp the work well enough to make good enough grades to go to college, then they need to start exploring all the trades that high school has to offer. If college is not for you, then go to trade school and specialize in a particular trade. The acquisition of specialized training often provides a greater income. Some people who learn a trade make more money than people with college degrees.

In America, there are so many programs to help individuals find a job. It is just a matter of doing continual research. Internet websites are great sources of information. Programs such as Work Source (a government-base program), help such individuals. God has blessed each person with abilities. It is up to each individual to seek out what God would have them do.

In the narrative about the talents God gave to each based on their ability (Matthew 25:14-18), He expected for them to gain more based on their ability. He did not take away any of their blessings. He added to their blessings based on what they had achieved (Matthew 25:28-29). *"I know that there is nothing better for them than to rejoice and to do good in one's lifetime; moreover, that every man who eats and drinks sees good in all his labor — it is the gift of God."* (Ecclesiastes 3:12-14; NASU)

Another passage of scripture which may help us to overcome poverty is, *"Then the word of the LORD came by Haggai the prophet, saying, "Is it time for you yourselves to dwell in your paneled houses while this house lies desolate?" Now therefore, thus says the LORD of hosts, Consider your ways! You have sown much, but harvest little; you eat, but there is not enough to be satisfied; you drink, but there is not enough to become drunk; you put on clothing, but no one is warm enough; and he who earns, earns wages to put into a purse with holes. Thus says the LORD of hosts, Consider your ways! Go up to the mountains, bring wood and rebuild the temple, that I may be pleased with it and be glorified, says the LORD. You look for much, but behold, it comes to little; when you bring it home, I blow it away. Why? declares the LORD of hosts, Because of My house which lies desolate, while each of you runs to his own house. Therefore, because of you the sky has withheld its dew and the earth has withheld its produce. I called for a drought on the land, on the mountains, on the grain, on the new wine, on the oil, on what the ground produces, on men, on cattle, and on all the labor of your hands."* (Haggai 1:3-11 NASU)

This passage shows us that poverty and financial difficulty can also occur due to our attitudes towards God. The suffering that was experienced before and during the one year ministry of Haggai was not a result of Satan attacking God's people. It was God who interfered with the financial well-being of the Israelites because of how they responded to the needs of the Lord's house. God makes it clear that their focus was selfish. *"It is time for you yourselves to dwell in your paneled houses while this house lies desolate?"* (Haggai 1:4)

God demonstrated patience by waiting sixteen years before having Haggai preach about this persistent problem. Remember that giving to God is clearly outlined in the Mosaic Law. God was so disturbed by their lack of obedience and commitment that he calls them 'this people.' (Haggai 1:2) The people could not figure out why during this time they were experiencing droughts, bad harvests, wages going out as fast as they were coming in, and their clothes never being sufficient for the changing weather.

This would all change if the people had put God first by deciding to rebuild God's house. God desires that we not only give to him first, in order to be blessed, but we must also make service to Him a priority. *"Honor the Lord with your wealth, and from the first of all your produce; so that your barns will be filled with plenty and your vats will overflow with new wine."* (Proverbs 3:10). *"Give, and it will be given to you. They will pour into your lap a good measure — pressed down, shaken together, and running over. For by your standard of measure it will be measured to you in return."* (Luke 6:38; NASU)

We must not only give to God from our wealth, but we must also give him our time. Each believer has a spiritual gift (1 Peter 4:10). We must employ our gifts by putting them to work in the church. Christ uses this process to fit his body together (Ephesians 4:12, 16). It is when this process is fully working that the body of Christ is powerfully activated to impact the community and the world (1 Corinthians 12; Ephesians 1:22-23) for the glory of God.

Just as our abilities determine our purpose in the world (2 Thessalonians 3:10), our spiritual gifts define our purpose in the church and empower the propagation of God's agenda. Serving in the local church blesses us. When we apply our God-given abilities, this allows us to get into the heart of everyone's everyday life to be salt and light to the world (Mathew 5:13-16). In addition, we will be blessed by God, because He rewards us through this process (Colossians 3:22-24).

A lady once asked John Wesley that if he knew that he would die at 12:00 midnight tomorrow, how would he spend the intervening time. His reply, "Why madam, just as I intend to spend it now. I would preach this evening at Gloucester, and again at five tomorrow morning; after that I would ride to Tewkesbury, preach in the afternoon, and meet the societies in the evening. I would then go to Rev. Martin's house, who expects to entertain me, talk and pray with the family as usual, retire to my room at 10 0'clock, commend myself to my heavenly father, lie down to rest, and wake up in Glory."

Haggai 1:9 says that they *'looked for much but behold it comes to little and when you bring it home I will blow it away.'* Note that it is God who is allowing this not Satan. The Lord of host instructs that the problem is a direct result of the ways (Haggai 1:5) of the people in Judah. People must consider their ways because His house lies desolate while they care for their own houses.

The desire to make our business of greater importance than the Lord's is not only damaging to the many who neglect Him, it is also damaging to our community and the country. Haggai 1:10 says, *"And I called for a drought on the land, on the mountains, on the grain, on the new wine, on the oil, on what they ground produces, on men, on cattle and on all the labor of your hands."*

Sodom and Gomorrah did not suffer because there was much sin in the land; it also suffered because God could not find ten righteous. The righteous knew sinners were sinning and were not willing to do anything. When the economy is slipping, home mortgages are climbing, jobs are getting hard to find, and people are hungry, it is not because of sinners, it is because of those who know God and choose to live a self centered lifestyle.

God's people cannot ignore God's kingdom work and expect God to not be concerned about their lack of commitment to service. God's people are the salt and light to the world (Matthew 5:13-16). If we look around us, do we see poverty? Are there people around the church that are unsaved? Are there people around the church that are not educated? Are there drunks and drug addicts on the street? What is the church doing to combat these problems? Some church buildings are falling apart, but what are we doing about it?

In Luke 4:18-19, He said; *"The Spirit of the Lord is upon Me, because He anointed Me to preach the gospel to the poor. He has sent Me to proclaim release to the captives and recovery of sight to the blind, to set free those who are downtrodden, to proclaim the favorable year of the Lord."* If there are needs throughout the church's community and the city leaders and believers are not doing anything about it, then we are not functioning in the will of God. Many times distress is upon believers not because of Satan, but because we refuse to give God time for service (2 Chronicles 15:2-7).

God specifically told us in Haggai that when we want to see blessings poured into our homes, we must take the house of God seriously. We must commit ourselves to treating God's house not only as a worship center, but also as a means through which God's agenda impacts the community and the world. Despite the fact that a person may work hard everyday and do everything it takes to be prosperous, God is saying that He will allow various circumstances to make life stressful, if we do not honor God's house.

In Luke 12:31, God instructs us to seek His kingdom first, and then He will address our needs. It does not say, "I will inspire you to seek it or anoint you to seek it," but instead obey me and seek it (Proverbs 2:1-7). From Luke 12:22-30, it tells us that clothes and all that we have need of will be added unto us. The Word tells us that God gladly blesses us 'according to His riches in glory.' (Philippians 4:19)

God's desire is to bless us and open up the windows of heaven and pour out blessings. We cannot rob Him (Malachi 3). Therefore, we must put God first. We must not let the left over money from our budgets be what you put in the offering plate. We should give from our first fruits. This is what Abel did, unlike his brother Cain. He gave God the firstlings of his flock and of his fat portions. (Genesis 4:4)

In Luke 12:33, He says go to work, sell your possessions, give to charities and make yourselves purses that do not wear out. In Haggai, He is saying that He will dig a hole in the purse, if we do not seek Him first. However, when we seek Him, He will sew up the hole in the purse. He will also give us purses that do not wear out. We will receive blessings that no thief can steal and no moth can destroy.

In Matthew 25, we find that He blessed the person that took care of the poor and the homeless, clothed the naked, took care of those who were hungry, and visited those who are in prison. There is even eternal punishment for unfaithful service for God's kingdom agenda. (Matthew 25:30) In Revelation, Christ responded the same way to lukewarm Christians. He says there are some that are very diligent, but they are sluggards when it comes to God. They are diligent about their own wealth. When people are diligent and do what is right and just, God blesses them. These people are blessed and prosperous, but they are sluggards to the church.

"I know your deeds, that you are neither cold nor hot; I wish that you were cold or hot. So because you are lukewarm, and neither hot nor cold, I will spit you out of My mouth. Because you say, "I am rich, and have become wealthy, and have need of nothing," and you do not know that you are wretched and miserable and poor and blind and naked...." (Revelation 3:15-18; NASU) Many believers forget that faithfulness in leadership can lead to great personal blessings. *"For those who have served well as deacons obtain for themselves a high standing and great confidence in the faith that is in Christ Jesus."* (1 Timothy 3:13).

The solution to our financial stress is not just working more overtime or getting better paying jobs. In fact, sometimes more money from a job brings more stress. It does not make sense to work hard when it goes right back out the door because God is putting holes in purses, allowing droughts to be created, and allowing wars to occur. To build a house without God is to build it in vain (Psalm 127).

The first action we must take is to commit to live by the standards of God and to faithfully work in His church (Ephesians 4:12), using our spiritual gifts (1 Peter 4:10; every believer has a gift). We must give faithfully, so that whatever we do it is done for the glory of God (1 Corinthians 10:31;

Colossians 3:17). If a person is working hard and looking prosperous but not putting God first, when life becomes difficult, then situations become even more complicated (1 Peter 3-9).

A prominent American, who was visiting Argentina, was asked by the president of the republic, "Why has South America gotten on so poorly and North America so well? What do you think is the reason?" The visitor replied, "I think the reason is the fact that the Spaniards came to South America seeking gold, while the Pilgrim Fathers came to North America seeking God."

God will find a way to break us down so that every time we fix the roof, the washing machine will break. Every time we fix the washing machine, the car will start smoking. When we fix the smoking car, our salary will get cut. We will always be pouring out the money as fast as we can make it. God is saying it is not the job that is taking care of us, that He is the one that is providing for us through the job.

In the Bible, the women who only gave one mite were richer, because she gave her one hundred percent which is obviously her very best. The woman who was gathering sticks to make a fire to cook her last meal before she and her sons died was blessed beyond measure because she chose to help God's prophet Elijah (1 Kings 1:17:8-16).

God was placed first even when poverty was about to lead to death. God is our provider whether we are walking through the wilderness on the way to the Promise Land or working everyday in the Promise Land. *"All the commandments that I am commanding you today you shall be careful to do, that you may live and multiply, and go in and possess the land which the LORD swore to give to your forefathers."* (Deuteronomy 8:1-2; NASU)

As believers, we must place God first in all we do. It is time for us to make the Lord's day the Lord's day. When we reverence Him and put Him first, we will overcome poverty as a church, as individuals and as a community. There is work to do and God will come and rip away all of our blessings if He is not placed first in our lives as He does not like being second. Believers can overcome poverty today, by utilizing our individual talents for the Glory of God.

CHAPTER 3

Gods Formula for Prosperity

The world has trained us to resort to different schemes and methods as a means of gaining prosperity. Although the worldly methods appear to produce some success stories; that does not mean that these methods are right. The world encourages people to gamble and to gain wealth by luck and chance. However, God instructs us to work in order to gain wealth. From the beginning of time, even before sin entered into the world, God placed Adam and Eve in the Garden of Eden to tend to the garden. (Genesis 2:15)

It is from a man's labor that God blesses him. Satan has always reversed everything from God's original intent. After Christ had fasted forty days and forty nights, Satan sought to tempt Him by asking him to turn stone into bread. Satan wanted Christ to change the stone to bread for His own well being and prosperity. Christ chose not to change God's way even though He was very hungry. He would rather have starved than go against God's authority. If God wanted the stone to be bread, He would have changed it and given it to Christ. After the temptation angels came and ministered to Christ to reestablish His strength for another day (Mark 1:13). Satan knew that Christ had the power to change the stone.

In fact, we actually use the power that God has given us to change things everyday. We tend to take the simple principles that God has taught us about working to provide for our families and we become influenced by the world's get rich schemes so that we do not have to work. This is actually a trick of the devil. *"The seed which fell among the thorns, these are the ones who have heard, and as they go on their way they are choked with worries and riches and pleasures of this life, and bring no fruit to maturity."* (Luke 8:14; NASU) This is why Solomon who had all the riches of the world said; *"He who trusts in his riches will fall, but the righteous will flourish like the green leaf."* (Proverbs 11:28; NASU)

Some people actually believe that they have the power within themselves to get rich. These individuals are so committed to being rich that it does not matter if they turn the stone into bread. A person who gains wealth in this manner has much sorrow. *"A faithful man will abound with blessings, but he who makes haste to be rich will not go unpunished."* (Proverbs 28:20; NASU) *"But those who want to get rich fall into temptation and a snare and many foolish and harmful desires which plunge men into ruin and destruction."* (1 Timothy 6:9-10; NASU)

God intends to bless believers. If we take the time to wait on God and follow His principles, He establishes His people, for our blessing, and for His glory and honor. God does not mind us being wealthy, but He wants to establish His system so that when we do receive prosperity, we do not receive it with selfish motives. God wants us to receive wealth in a way that keeps His kingdom purposes and plans moving forward.

Therefore, as stated in 1 Timothy we must *"Instruct those who are rich in this present world not to be conceited or to fix their hope on the uncertainty of riches, but on God, who richly supplies us with all things to enjoy. Instruct them to do good, to be rich in good works, to be generous and ready to share, storing up for themselves the treasure of a good foundation for the future, so that they may take hold of that which is life indeed."* (1 Timothy 6:17-19; NASU)

"Perhaps the most gem-adorned woman in history was Lollia Paullina, third wife of Emperor Caligula. She inherited the immense fortune from her grandfather who amassed it through vice and corruption. The Elder Pliny reported seeing her at a modest dinner party loaded down with emeralds and pearls worth $36 million dollars today. In order that her gem-laden reputation might remain undisputed, she always carried with her the bills of sale to prove her claim." (Tan, 1979) *"By wisdom a house is built, And by understanding it is established; And by knowledge the rooms are filled with all precious and pleasant riches. A wise man is strong, And a man of knowledge increases power.*" (Prov 24:3-5; NASU)

This chapter addresses the difference between God making us wealthy and the world making us wealthy. When we choose to let Him develop the wealth, it becomes His formula for righteousness and blessings. Ecclesiastes 5: 19 -20 states, *"Furthermore, as for every man to whom God has given riches and wealth, He has also empowered him to eat from them and to receive his reward and rejoice in his labor; this is the gift of God. For he will not often consider the years of his life, because God keeps him occupied with the gladness of his heart."* (NASU)

In the Bible, riches are the accumulation of things and wealth is the state of comprehensively doing well and being physically healthy. What the Bible also means by wealth, is that whatever riches we have are being multiplied in all kinds of ways to make more riches. Wealth is a comprehensive richness in terms of health, spirituality, emotional strength and the accumulation of material goods. This is why when God supplies this kind of wealth, it leads to righteousness. The scripture goes on to say that He has *'empowered him to eat from them and to receive his reward.'* In other words, when God makes us rich and healthy we will receive our reward from it.

This is why we must follow God's formula for prosperity. Even though it may take more discipline, it is most definitely more productive. We cannot receive blessings of wealth until we learn to rejoice in our labor. Ecclesiastes 3:22 states *"I have seen that nothing is better than that man should be happy in his activities, for that is his lot. For who will bring him to see what will occur after him?"*

The gift of God comes when people rejoice in your labor. In Psalms 128:5 God says that these individuals will not consider the years of their life because they will become abundant and live long. *"The LORD bless you from Zion, and may you see the prosperity of Jerusalem all the days of your life. Indeed, may you see your children's children. Peace be upon Israel"* (Psalms 128:5-6; NASU) God keeps these individuals occupied with the gladness in their hearts, which reduces stress and leads to long life.

There are some people who do not just want to get rich, they actually love money. These individuals become victims of a worldly mindset. 1 Timothy Ch. 6 teaches what goes wrong when individuals seek to follow the formula of the world and seek to turn the stone to bread. In 1 Timothy 6:9, *"But those who want to get rich will fall into temptation and a snare and many foolish and harmful desires will now plunge them into ruin and destruction."*

Just because a person has a lot of money, it does not mean that the person loves money. However, those who love money, and are controlled by a strong desire to always have money, are often led into evil acts. The Bible teaches us that the love of money makes these individuals neglect God. For instance, when people have the resources to give to God, and do not give, then they love money. *"No one can serve two masters; for either he will hate the one and love the other, or he will hold to one and despise the other. You cannot serve God and mammon"* (money; Matthew 6:24).

The challenge at the offering plate is the issue of who do believers trust most. The love of money is the root of all sorts of evil. If the love of money drives a person to gamble, then that person may stay at the casino all night if he or she believes this is necessary to gain more money.

The love of money can also affect relationships within our homes. Many marriages struggle, because some couples spend too much time trying to get rich and not enough quality time with one another. Then the money runs the house and not love. The kids get caught in the snare, because they have to have all the brand name products and the latest items in technology. As a result, the longing for money causes some people to wander away and give up on God. This causes their lives to get worse and leads to these individuals being plagued with many more troubles.

Ray Jones once wrote a poem called; "A Dollar Speaks." "Money talks, we have been told since childhood. Listen to this dollar speak: You hold me in your hand and call me yours. Yet may I not as well call you mine. See how easily I rule you? To gain me, you would all but die. I am invaluable as rain, essential as water. Without me, men and institutions would die. Yet I do not hold the power of life for them; I am futile without the stamp of your desire. I go nowhere unless you send me. I keep strange company. For me, men mock, love, and scorn character. Yet, I am appointed to the service of saints, to give education to the growing mind and food to the starving bodies of the poor. My power is terrific. Handle me carefully and wisely, lest you become my servant, rather than I yours." (Tan, 1979)

However, the person who follows God's formula for prosperity, rather than the world's formula, will be blessed. God's formula is a process of spirituality, not a get rich scheme. The person that chooses to get rich following the ways of the world will not experience long term benefit.

This does not mean that these individuals would not have money, but in the end Satan uses the world's process to devour them. Remember that Satan loves to imitate Christ (2 Corinthians 11:14) and he seeks to be a shepherd.

Unfortunately he is not a good shepherd because he seeks to kill, steal and destroy (John 10: 1-2, 10). Unlike Satan's process, God's process is one that powerfully impacts a person's character and well being. God's wealth always sustains and blesses each individual who patiently submits to his formula.

First of all, God's formula for success involves hard work (this does not mean long hours) and patience. Proverbs 28:19 tells us, *"He who tills the land will have plenty of food."* The word 'till' is a gardening term which means to cultivate the soil. When a person tills the ground, he or she plows the land until it is perfectly ready for sowing seed. Successful gardeners provide great principles for us to follow when showing diligence in our labor. Gardeners first take care of the ground itself. They till the ground in order to break up the dirt to prepare it for planting. They may also treat the soil with topsoil or growth enhancers before planting their crops.

Just like gardening, we must take our schooling seriously. If a person does not feel they are college material, they should learn a trade and seek to progress in learning all they can with a trade. While learning the trade, they can try to find a job that challenges them to apply what they are learning. While on the job, they may have to start at the ground level and work hard there before promoted to the next level. This also applies to a person with a college degree, in that while studying, they may take the summer months to find internships. This allows them to till the land while getting a degree.

Once the ground has been properly prepared for planting, the gardener then plants his crops. When the crops are planted, the gardener must water and tend to the garden frequently in order for the crops to grow. If the gardener does not do this, the crops will not grow healthy and vibrant. Similar to gardening, when we are promoted to the next level, above ground level, we must continue to work hard and be faithful on our jobs in order to gain prosperity.

As a result of the gardener's faithfulness, not only at the ground level, but during the growth process, he or she will reap the benefits of what has been sewn. 2 Corinthians 9:6 states, *"Remember this: whoever sows sparingly will also reap sparingly, and whoever sows generously will also reap generously."* A farmer who plants a few seeds will get only a small crop, but he who plants much, he will reap much. If we want to gain prosperity, we must also plant seeds on good ground and reap our harvests through hard work and dedication. When we provide honest, hard work on our jobs, God will cause our jobs to produce blessings beyond measure. Proverbs 28:19 says; *"he who tills his land will have plenty of food, but he who follows empty pursuits will have poverty in plenty."* ~A lazy man does not roast his prey, but he precious possession of a *man is diligence."* (Proverbs. 12:27) *"The should of the sluggard craves and get nothing, but the soul of the diligent is made fat."* (Proverbs. 13:4).

God blesses us as a result of our faithful labor. I grew up in a family that believed that whatever your hands find to do, make sure it is done well the first time, with all of your might. (Ecclesiastes 9:10). One of the things that causes us not to be blessed is that many of us show up to work and do not want to work because we may not like the job or it does not pay much. The Bible teaches us that if we are faithful with a few things, we will be placed in charge of many more things (Matthew 25:21).

God uses our faithfulness with a little to bless us with more. What kind of steward would give more to us when we are faithful with a few things? For God to continue to give to us would mean that He is a bad steward of His resources. *"Let a man regard us in this manner, as servant of Christ and stewards of the mysteries of God. In this case, moreover, it is required of stewards that one be found trustworthy."*(1 Corinthians 4:1-3) Therefore, we must make good use of whatever we are blessed with by God blesses. Some businesses pay for employees to go to school or to get specialized training. We should seize the opportunities on our job, knowing that God has placed us in positions to bless us.

In 2 Thessalonians 3:10, the Word teaches that if a man does not work then he should not eat.

That is why when a physically healthy man does not work and asks for benevolence we say no, because if this person gets hungry enough they will find a way to eat. A lady came to me and said that her husband did not want to work and did not want to look for a job. I asked her why he was in her house.

In the Garden of Eden when Adam sinned God did not let him enjoy the luxury of the garden, but He kicked him out. I do not believe in divorce but you can separate because if a person is sinning and does not have a repentant heart the Bible says to remove them (Matthew 18:15-20; 1 Corinthians 5; Marriage is representative of Christ and the church, Ephesians 5:32). My advice to her was to kick him out because there were little boys in the house thinking that it was okay to have a woman and not work. This would show those young boys that if they do not work then they will not eat.

Some people want to be blessed by God, but we do not want to work. Some want to show up to work late and then ask God to keep their jobs. Some people will do poor or mediocre work but ask for a raise or a promotion. The first step to God's formula is to work. We are in a generation of people that do not want to work. We will try any get rich scheme just to keep from working. When God made Adam he told him to work because he was going to have dominion over the earth. You cannot have dominion, if you are not doing anything. The children of Israel ended up staying in the wilderness and dying because they were always complaining (1 Corinthians 10:9-13).

God said that this was an example for us to save us from destruction. However, when God made man he made him naturally physically stronger than a woman and he made him with the physical capacity to work. God commanded the man to work. The woman as a man's helper can decide to work, but a man is designed to work. Working for a living is not a result of sin, it has always been the plan of God (Genesis 2:15; "cultivate the garden").

Satan would love to reverse it and have the woman work and the man stay at home. In Colossians, it tells us to obey our masters in the earth not with external service as those that merely please men, but with sincerity of heart pleasing God. We are not to fear the boss or the supervisor because God says that we will have plenty when we till the soil. God will make our soil productive and fertile because we commit to obey him. Our rewards will come from our work. In Proverbs it says a faithful man will abound in blessing (Proverbs 28:10).

The second component of God's formula for prosperity requires us to become good stewards of our money. In Proverbs 3:9, Solomon instructs several young men to be faithful stewards so that they would experience prosperity. In Proverbs 3:10, He told them to honor the Lord with their wealth. This verse is not speaking just about giving. This passage uses the word 'honor' which means to make God happy. In the Old Testament this word does not mean respect, but it means to become heavy. This means that we are so burdened with a desire to obey God's principles that whatever we do with our money must be guided by decisions that please Him.

How we spend our money should be dominated by God. In Romans it instructs us on how to be good stewards over God's money. The book of Romans addresses the issue of taxes. In general, people do not like to pay taxes. Romans 13:1-2 states *"Everyone must submit himself to the governing authorities , for there is no authority except that which God has established. The authorities that exist have been established by God. Consequently, he who rebels against the authority is rebelling against what God has instituted, and those who do will bring judgment on themselves."* In the book of Luke, it tells us to give Caesar what belongs to Caesar and give God what belongs to God (Luke 20:25).

In order to be good stewards of our money, we must pay our taxes. We cannot drive on the freeway, or get benefits without paying taxes. We will try to get around 'Uncle Sam,' but when we get older and do not have any money; we would then ask God to bless us. We must render to all that is due. We should not accumulate bills that we cannot pay. If God blesses us with a little car, then we need to thank Him for that. We should be faithful in how we take care of the car. Clean it, change the oil on time, and rotate the tires to get all we can out of them.

God is saying that in order for Him to bless us we must be good stewards with whatever he provides and pay what is due. Too many people function without a budget. I have seen people with no plan and when things do not go right they blame God. They say 'Lord I gave my dollar now give me fifty.' However, He wants us to become good stewards over the money that He blesses us with. If God tells us to pay taxes, then we must pay taxes. If we borrow money, then we must pay it back. When we come to church we must demonstrate that we trust Him to be our Provider and give as He has instructed us. When giving to God, we must give to Him from our first fruits. It should be the first check we write, not the last one after paying all our bills.

Proverbs 3:9 teaches us *"to honor the Lord with our wealth, with the first fruit of our crops."* God is not going to bless someone that is not being a good steward. In the practice of good stewardship, we should not over extend ourselves financially. For instance, it is better to have a small simple car that runs well, than to have a fancy car that you cannot pay for. It is better to live in a small house with a low mortgage than to have a big house that you cannot even afford to furnish. It is better to go grocery shopping and take time to cook than to eat fast food everyday. We end up destroying our budgets by eating fast food so frequently. Then the fast food often destroys our bodies and this leads to huge medical bills. Formulate a budget, based on the principles of God, and then discipline the entire family to live within it.

Paul summarized the mindset that we should have when he said *"But I rejoiced in the Lord greatly, that now at last you have revived your concern for me; indeed, you were concerned before, but you lacked opportunity. Not that I speak from want, for I have learned to be content in whatever circumstances I am. I know how to get along with humble means, and I also know how to live in prosperity; in any and every circumstance I have learned the secret of being filled and going hungry, both of having abundance and suffering need. I can do all things through Him who strengthens me."* (Philippians 4:10-13; NASU)

He accepted the circumstances that God allowed him to experience and remained focused on fulfilling God's agenda for his life. *"For I am already being poured out as a drink offering, and the time of my departure has come. I have fought the good fight, I have finished the course, I have kept the faith; in the future there is laid up for me the crown of righteousness, which the Lord, the righteous Judge, will award to me on that day; and not only to me, but also to all who have loved His appearing."* (1 Timothy 4:6-8)

God's third part of the formula for prosperity requires that we get out of debt. The Word instructs us to 'owe nothing to anyone.'

"Owe nothing to anyone except to love one another; for he who loves his neighbor has fulfilled the law." (Romans 13:8-9; NASU) God is telling us to work hard to get out of debt, because if we do not, we become a slave to our debtors. Even though the focus of the narrative in Matthew 18:21-35 is about forgiveness it is still clear that the two men who owed money were slaves to their debtors. This was even worse in their day, because the owner could even take a person's children to work off the debt (2 Kings 4:1).

Many people try to live above their means. In addition, many people determine how prosperous a person is, not based on how they structured their money Biblically, but by what their money can buy. This is why we should not *'compare ourselves with some of those who commend themselves; but when they measure themselves by themselves, and compare themselves with themselves, they are without understanding."* (2 Corinthians 10:12-13).

God wants to bless us, but it has to be within in His formula. Pay off debt first by never getting into so much debt that you cannot pay more on a credit card or on your mortgage than the amount that is required. Try to make at least one extra mortgage payment a year and if you can afford it, get a 15-year mortgage rather than a 30-year mortgage. If you have to get a credit card never get a credit card that has high interest rates. Some single parents find it difficult to operate their homes without a credit card. If you must get a credit card get only one card not two or more. Some people say get a good used car, but this does not make too much sense to me. I would rather get a new small car that fits well within my budget with a three year note. Maintain it well and try to pay if off a few months early. Pay off the small bills first and then take these resources to pay off the larger bills.

Once out of debt, focus on organizing your budget to take care of retirement and build an emergency savings account for incidentals such as tire blow outs, appliance repairs, etc. In addition, have a savings account that is in place in case you are laid off or get sick for an extended period of time. You may even seek to get disability insurance in case you are sick for a long period of time. Above all these, give to God first. We must consistently demonstrate a dependence on God to be our Provider. *"There is one who scatters, and yet increases all the more, and there is one who withholds what is justly due, and yet it results only in want. The generous man will be prosperous, and he who waters will himself be watered."* (Proverbs 11:24-25; NASU) Structuring our budgets to do the things God has commanded us to do, places the 'burden' on God to honor His word and bless us with prosperity.

When we are faithful, God can bless us even when we are sleeping. He also blesses us based on how we seek Him or fear Him (Luke

12:31-32; Psalm 128). I remember not being paid for three months from the Bible College for which I once worked. I was in need of money to send my wife to Canada to see her family whom she had not seen in six years. I told the Lord that I have worked and have tilled the soil and that He had to produce it. I was asleep one Saturday afternoon, after working outside and the phone rang and the person on the other end said that I had been on their mind for a week. They said that they had a thousand dollars left in their mission's budget that they were going to bless us with. I remember jumping up and down constantly repeating 'thank you Lord, thank you Lord!' I felt so responsible for helping my wife see her family because when we got married she moved to where I lived.

His word tells us that God rewards faith (Hebrews 11:6). Faithfully abiding in His Word moves us from experiencing what we need to being blessed with want we desire. *"I am the vine, you are the branches; he who abides in Me and I in him, he bears much fruit, for apart from Me you can do nothing. If anyone does not abide in Me, he is thrown away as a branch and dries up; and they gather them, and cast them into the fire and they are burned. If you abide in Me, and My words abide in you, ask whatever you wish, and it will be done for you. My Father is glorified by this, that you bear much fruit, and so prove to be My disciples. Just as the Father has loved Me, I have also loved you; abide in My love."* (John 15:5-10; NASU) When we abide in Christ, through the

Word of God, our minds are renewed (Romans 12:2) and His perfect will becomes ours. When His perfect will is our will, blessing us brings God glory. A person does not lose following this process.

We can become prosperous by God's process or by the world's process. The world's way of achieving prosperity is temporary, but God's way is eternal. The world's system is attractive and seems to bring fast results, but it totally depends on results. However, God's system is based on God's faithfulness and therefore it is under His constant support whether we are in need or are doing well. He promises to never leave us nor will He forsake us (Matthew 28:20).

"My sheep hear My voice, and I know them, and they follow Me; and I give eternal life to them, and they will never perish; and no one will snatch them out of My hand. My Father, who has given them to Me, is greater than all; and no one is able to snatch them out of the Father's hand. I and the Father are one." (John 10:27-30; NASU) We gain everything when we submit our lives to the will of God rather than the ways of a world that functions contrary to God.

C H A P T E R 4

Treasure Seekers vs. Treasure Keepers

Most people are faced with the need to provide for their families. This need can create a great deal of pressure for many families. The pressure sometimes leads to divorce. In fact, financial pressure serves as one of the leading reasons couples separate. Financial pressure oftentimes causes people to become treasure seekers.

Many churches have catered to this need by encouraging Christians to believe that God wants to bless all believers with wealth. In other words, every Christian is supposed to be rich, and if they are not, there must be something wrong with their faith. There is not a person who does not have a need to pay bills and maintain a balanced budget. So this concept that is preached sometimes creates greater pressure when families are tithing, attending church consistently, and are faithfully trying to apply the principles being taught, but yet their financial state is still not perfect.

In reality, it is not true that everyone is going to be rich because they are saved. As a matter of fact, Christ, while on earth, did not leave His disciples or His apostles with great wealth. The apostle Paul was so poor that he said; *"Not that I speak from want, for I have learned to be content in whatever circumstances I am. I know how to get along with humble means, and I also know how to live in prosperity; in any and every circumstance I have learned the secret of being filled and going hungry, both of having abundance and suffering need. I can do all things through Him who strengthens me."* (Phil 4:10-14; NASU)

The same was true for Christ's disciple, Peter. When a beggar saw Peter going into the temple, he requested that Peter give him money. *"But Peter said, "I do not possess silver and gold, but what I do have I give to you: In the name of Jesus Christ the Nazarene — walk!"* (Acts 3:6; NASU) In another instance, when Judas confronted Christ about allowing the woman to use costly perfume to wash Christ's feet, Christ said to Judas, the poor will always be among you (John 12:8). In yet another instance, when the man wanted to follow Jesus because maybe he thought that this would make his life better, Jesus told him, *"The foxes have holes and the birds of the air have nests, but the Son of Man has nowhere to lay His head."* (Luke 9:58-59; NASU)

In each of these passages Jesus shows us that he does not intend to make us rich because we give our lives to Him. However, some Christian groups go to the extreme with the idea of being poor because scripture mentions on several occasions that we will have trials. These groups imply in their teachings that we must be willing to suffer with Christ to reign with Christ (Romans 8:18). So in the midst of all of the doctrinal differences, and financial pressure, what is God saying?

The truth is, God does not desire that every Christian become rich, or that every Christian live in poverty. God has never promised to make all of us rich. He actually instructs us not to love the things of the world (1 John 2:15-17) or to love money, because to be mastered by it is to not have him as our master (Proverbs 5:10; 1 Timothy 6:10; Matthew 6:24). The love of the things of this world can prevent spiritual growth (Luke 8:14), create conflict (James 4:1-3), cause our prayers to be ineffective, and lead us to become enemies of God.

This is probably why in Proverbs 30:7, the writer is asking God to keep deception and lies from him and give him neither poverty nor riches. He is asking God to fill him with the food that is his portion, unless he becomes full and deny Him, or be rich and forsake Him. He is saying Lord do not make me poor so that I will not steal, lie or do wrong in order to achieve a sense of livelihood. He is also saying God do not make me rich, because then I may say who is God that I should need Him. However, he is asking God to give him middle ground so that he neither forsakes Him in his lifestyle because of being poor, nor forsakes Him because he is rich and may feel independent of God.

In the Garden of Eden, Adam had everything. God came to meet with him and spend time with him. Adam owned everything and had dominion over everything, but that turned out to not be enough. Eve, who was influenced by Satan, wanted to be just like God. *"For God knows that in the day you eat from it your eyes will be opened, and you will be like God, knowing good and evil."* (Genesis 3:5) This selfish ambition led Adam to sin.

When Adam trusted in the words of another, he rejected the words of God. By doing this, Adam was demonstrating independence from God and rebellion to God. However, Adam still needed God. This decision made life harder and more difficult to sustain because he now had to live, under God's powerful influence on everything. Work moved from being a joy to being a burden (Genesis 3:17-19).

The problem today is that people have become obsessed with the 'garden' (the resources God has allow mankind to enjoy), rather than the Gardener. When the Gardener demands obedience, submission, time, and giving, many of us do not respond, because we believe that the Garden (earth and all its resources) can supply all our needs. Mankind operates as if all he needs is for God to keep everything in order and then people can take care of the rest. Instead of enjoying the purpose of the garden, because of a relationship with the Gardener, man ends up enjoying the garden for a moment (1 John 2:17).

Some of us come to Christ as if we expect for Him to be a 'Sugar Daddy.' We are asking God to give and give, and bless and bless. However, we cannot achieve success or wealth, until we develop a growing relationship with Christ (Joshua 1:6-9; Proverbs 24:3-5). When we develop a growing relationship with Christ, then we become treasure keepers, rather than treasure seekers.

We are more righteous when we do not seek to enjoy the riches from the world, but instead when we seek to enjoy a healthy relationship with Christ (James 5:16). This healthy relationship creates a friendship with Christ (John 15:14), and leads to Christ granting our desires (John 15:7). *"I have been young and now I am old, yet I have not seen the righteous forsaken or his descendants begging bread."* (Psalms 37:25; NASU)

The fact is, God placed Christ on Calvary to win mankind back to Himself. When we accept this offer, it reveals all that God has for us. The more we develop our relationship with God, because we develop a greater understanding of His Word and are willing to obey it, the more we experience all His benefits. The more intimate the experience, the greater the trust, and the greater the trust, the more powerfully God functions for us. (Hebrews 11:6) Without God, man can do nothing (John 15:5). When man lives independent of God, he functions like a man who has no money, but has good credit with a bank, but chooses not to utilize the bank's services. When man lives without God, every day is a greater struggle because he bears no fruit.

When man functions independently of God, he demonstrates selfish ambition. If you want to be treasure keepers, rather than treasure seekers, then God must be involved in our decision-making. James 3:13-17 instructs us in this area by stating *"For where you have envy and selfish ambition, there you will find disorder and every evil practice. But the wisdom that comes from heaven is first of all pure; then peace-loving, considerate, submissive, full of mercy and good fruit, impartial and sincere."*

An instance in the Bible in which selfish ambition is clearly demonstrated, is found the book of Luke Ch. 12. During that time, when a father died, he would leave two-thirds of his inheritance to the oldest son because he had the responsibility of taking care of the mother and taking care of sisters who may have been unmarried. All the other sons received what was left. However, selfish ambition caused one brother to dispute this custom. Luke 12:13-15 says,

"Someone in the crowd said to Him, "Teacher, tell my brother to divide the family inheritance with me." But He said to him, " Man, who appointed Me a judge or arbitrator over you?" Then He said to them, " Beware, and be on your guard against every form of greed; for not even when one has an abundance does his life consist of his possessions." (Luke 12:13-15; NASU)

One would think that this man in Luke 12;13 would come to Jesus and ask him to make a wise decision about the problem concerning how the brother divided what was left. The inheritance had already been distributed, but he was unhappy. He was telling Jesus to convince his brother to divide the family inheritance with him. He was saying that he wanted more. This young man was not trying to please God, he was seeking to please himself. His discontentment was a result of his selfish ambition. However, Christ explains to him that abundance in life does not mean that one has an abundance of possessions. Jesus then explains how a rich man had a great crop and decided to build larger barns and *`store up grain and my goods. And I will say to my soul, "Soul you have many good laid up for many years to come; take your ease, eat, drink and be merry."* This man's selfish ambition and independence from God did not allow him to enjoy God's blessings (Luke 12:17-21).

It is not uncommon for many individuals today to feel a sense of discontentment in our financial state. Contentment does not come to us naturally. It is certainly a learned trait. This is an important characteristic to learn because it is a natural instinct for individuals to always want more. God could provide us with a nice house, and we may want more space in the house. Perhaps someone else buys a brick house and then we want a brick house. Maybe we see someone with a fine luxury car, and then we may want to sell our simple economical car to purchase a nicer car.

However, God cannot bless us until we learn how to be content. *"But godliness actually is a means of great gain when accompanied by contentment. For we have brought nothing into the world, so we cannot take anything out of it either. If we have food and covering, with these we shall be content. But those who want to get rich fall into temptation and a snare and many foolish and harmful desires which plunge men into ruin and destruction. For the love of money is a root of all sorts of evil, and some by longing for it have wandered away from the faith and pierced themselves with many griefs.* (1 Tim 6:6-10; NASU)

In 1 Timothy 6:6, it tells us that godliness, not a big paycheck, is where the contentment starts. When we obtain godliness, then we learn to walk with God according His standards, laws, and creeds. The reason why godliness leads to contentment is because it provides spiritual growth, which in turn teaches us to live dependent on God. (John 15:1-5) The more we mature spiritually, the more we experience peace and self control which are fruits of the Spirit. (Galatians 5:22-26) When we do not function under the Spirit's control, we remain influenced by the flesh. The lust of the flesh produces greed. (James 1:14-15) The flesh is never satisfied. That is why when individuals are controlled by the lust of the flesh, it can lead to the love of money, which soon becomes their master and leads them to *'harmful desires which plunge men into ruin and destruction"* (1 Timothy 6:9; Matthew 6:24). This is why Paul states *"those who are in the flesh cannot please God."* (Romans 8:8)

Greed is like the thirst of the man that drank salt water. The more he drank the more water he needed until he died. Goods were not designed to satisfy us. Only life fills life. We should seek God for wisdom, rather than for financial gain. In 1 Kings 3:5, the Lord appeared to Solomon in a dream and said, *"Ask for whatever you want me to give you."* Solomon did not ask for riches. Instead Solomon said *"So give your servant a discerning heart to govern your people and to distinguish between right and wrong."* (1 Kings 3:9)

The Lord was pleased that Solomon had asked for this. So God said to him, *'Since you have asked for this and not for long life and wealth for yourself, nor have you asked for the death of your enemies but for discernment in administering justice, I will do what you have asked. I will give you a wise and discerning heart, so that there will never have been anyone like you, nor will there ever be. Moreover, I will give you what you have not asked for—both riches and honor—so that your lifetime will have no equal among kings. And if you walk in my ways and obey my commands as David your father did, I will give you a long life."* (1 Kings 3:10-14) God is telling us to fall in love with Him and then the world's possessions will be of less value to us. God becomes our resource who provides us what we need (Luke 12:31-32), and what we desire (John 15:7).

The apostle Paul would say that for us to live is Christ and to die is gain. (Philippians 1:210) He could look back and count what he had in the past as a loss and what he obtained with Christ as gain. (Philippians 4:7-15) It is the lack of Christ that creates the hunger for worldly possessions. We should seek God to gain abundant life, rather than material possessions. This is why Christ states, *"The thief comes only to steal, and kill, and destroy; I came that they might have life, and might have it abundantly."* (John 10:10)

A relationship with God leads to contentment. The love of money is what led to the ruin and destruction of Judas. Judas had the opportunity to walk with Christ, and witness the powerful life of Christ, the great miracles He performed, and all of Christ's teachings. Due to his greed, Judas allowed money to become his master. When Jesus was at the pinnacle of His popularity, Judas saw how he could make more money, but not how he could use the money collected to impact more lives. This led to his destruction.

In the early 1960's, a man trained as a plumber participated in a small raw land purchase in West Houston. He developed houses, apartments and commercial property on the land. From the beginning, he continued to develop larger and more complex properties. He maintained virtually complete control and ownership of everything he built, from the raw land to a completed hospital, a major shopping mall, apartments, and office buildings. In short, he became fabulously wealthy.

He spared no expense on building his properties. They were high quality, though sometimes overly flashy and ostentatious with marble and chandeliers. When the buildings were completed, the landscaping was done all at once, with solid turf and detailed flowerbeds. Instead of little twigs for trees he planted mature trees. Instead of inexpensive, fast-growing trees, he often planted quality trees, like live oaks. The end result was a lovely landscape that appeared mature though brand new.

His financial success came at a price. He was known as an unpleasant, brutal businessman who enjoyed cutting his competitors, suppliers, and tenants off at the knees. This man seemed lost, without love, and unhappy. To his credit, his marriage lasted a lifetime. However, stories of the fruit of that marriage, his children, told of suicide, drugs, and heartache. He lived in chronic pain, due to failed back surgery and demanded many surgeries and procedures in a futile attempt at pain relief. He hoarded his money. For decades, he lived in a relatively small unattractive house with burglar bars. At one point, his house was literally in the shadow of one of his office buildings.

He was 85 when he died in 2000. He is buried in Memorial Oaks Cemetery in West Houston. His family has a plot that measures 20 x 70 feet. A nice marble border surrounds the edge of the plot. The plot is well landscaped, separate from the adjacent cemetery land. The cemetery grass is Saint Augustine, but inside the plot it is a well-fertilized thin stem golf course type grass. At the back of the plot is a small landscaped garden. Right in the middle of the garden is a nice sized live oak tree, obviously planted in that precise spot as a focal landscape detail. Fresh flowers are kept in vases over the family graves. Overall the plot looks chillingly similar in design, construction, and landscaping to his other projects.

Here then is the end of a man who was incredibly successful at gaining the wealth and glory of the world. This is the story of Joseph Johnson, the man who developed and owned Memorial City Shopping Center, Memorial City

Hospital, of Houston Texas, and many other properties. He led a tragic, self-centered life and was destructive to his family and those who dealt with him. He took particular pleasure in intimidating everyone around him, and seemed to get virtually no other pleasure from his wealth. (June 3, 1915 – December 13, 2000 Source: G B Mayes)

He was a legend in West Houston and many stories are told of his business skills, power, and wealth. However, no stories are told of his reverence to God, or his kindness towards his fellow man. He led a mean, unhappy life. His life clearly shows us that worldly possessions cannot bring us happiness. *"For what will it profit a man if he gains the whole world and forfeits his soul? "* *(Matthew 16:26) "The wages of the righteous is life, the income of the wicked, punishment."* (Proverbs 10:16)

In Luke 12:16-21, Christ tells the parable of a rich man. There are three valuable lessons that we can learn from this man's misconceptions about his richness. The first lesson is that we do not gain riches on our own. When Christ told the story of the rich man, He did not say that the man's business was not productive or that He did not do well. Christ states that the man's business did well. He was a farmer, which obviously means he, maybe unknowingly, depended on the goodness of God to send rain. If a person's business does well, they would need to build more places to store their crop. None of these decisions are unreasonable. There are two major issues in this passage that create the problem. The first one is that the rich man repeatedly used the personal pronoun "I". He viewed himself as self-sufficient just like King Nebuchadnezzar. In Luke 12:18 alone, he uses 'I' three times.

This is a trait that creates selfish ambition, which James says is *'earthly, natural, demonic'* (3:15c), and it creates *'disorder and every evil thing.'* (3:16c). The man did not realize that all good and perfect gifts comes from above (James 1:17). He viewed his wealth as a result of his work. He lived independent of God. However, in order to be treasure keepers, we must be dependent on God. In His word, he tells us, *"Abide in Me, and I in you. As the branch cannot bear fruit of itself unless it abides in the vine, so neither can you unless you abide in Me. "I am the vine, you are the branches; he who abides in Me and I in him, he bears much fruit, for apart from Me you can do nothing."* (John 15:4-5; NASU)

The second lesson that we can learn from this rich man, is that we must find security in God, and not in our finances. This man took the blessings of God to create his own sense of security. However, Christ emphasized humility and discouraged pride (seeking to live independent of God; 1 Peter 5:5-6). Those who depend on Him are blessed are in turn blessed. Even Jesus, who has the very nature of God (Hebrews 1:3), *"humbled Himself by becoming obedient to the point of death, even death on the cross."* (Philippians 2:8; Matthew 5:5) Understand though, that dependence on God does not mean that we do not plan for the future. There is nothing wrong with developing a retirement plan or having a savings account. However, we deceive ourselves when we believe that it is the money that is taking care of us.

To have a sense of security in something that cannot produce life and has no life in itself, is like trusting in a tree to give a person love. The tree is just a tree, so it lacks arms, a heart and a mind. It is impossible for a tree to provide love. It can only provide shade. For a person to believe that money can provide security is not different. Money cannot remove disease from a person's body, even though it can buy quality health insurance. Money may provide a car with airbags, but it cannot save a person's life in a tragic car crash. Money may provide a beautiful house, but it cannot create a home full of love. Money may take a person on a beautiful vacation, but it cannot control whether or not the plane will land. Money can provide a child an education, but it cannot guarantee the child would graduate. Money can, however, help to feed the hungry and cloth the naked.

This is why God instructs those who have money to not hoard it (1 Timothy 6:17-18). It is when a person uses money based on God's kingdom plan that it takes on life. When a people organize their resources based on the Word of God, money produces greater results. It builds a home, not just a house (Psalm 128; Proverbs 24:3-5). It blesses lives through missionaries who touch people around the world, or through a church which changes lives within the family and in the community. Work is no longer a curse, but it becomes a person's lot (Ecclesiastes 3:22; Colossians 3:23-25).

God tells us that we have brought nothing into the world and we cannot take anything out of it. When we chase after worldly possessions, then we lose life. Many children have the worldly possessions, like video games, clothes, toys and cars, but no life, because parents are not home enough to impart life. One of the things that the rich man needed to learn was contentment, before he could experience the blessings of God.

God wants us to first deal with our greed and learn contentment, because if we learn contentment, then we learn to trust Him. He is then the one who is guiding us, controlling us and blessing us. We must learn to be dependent on Him. In order to be a treasure keeper, we cannot be a treasure seeker. When one has an abundance of possessions, this does not necessarily bring security and happiness in life. No one who is gravely ill in the hospital is asking for a million dollars, but they are asking for help, because their focus is life.

God wants us to draw near to Him, not for the world, but to experience heaven on earth (Galatians 2:20; Colossians 3:1-4). How would you like to be in a relationship where the person only wants your stuff and not you? How do we think Jesus feels about this when He died on Calvary's cross to give us life, but yet we seek material goods. When Christ died on the cross, He did not put a bunch of material goods at the bottom of the cross and tell us to come and get those goods and then we would be saved. Instead, He was trying to give us godliness that would lead to contentment. He died and rose up from the grave, not because of man's goodness, but so that we may have life and have it abundantly as a result of a relationship with God (John 10:10). The fruit of this life is *"... love, joy, peace, patience, kindness, goodness, faithfulness, gentleness, self-control; against such things there is no law." (Gal 5:22-24; NASU)* None of these things money can buy.

A false sense of security leads us to view the blessings of God as our possessions. We begin to forget that all good and perfect gifts come from above. *"For we have brought nothing into the world, so we cannot take anything out of it either."* (1 Timothy 6:7) When we receive blessings from God, we must remember that they belong to God and He therefore has the right to say what we must do with them. We must receive our gifts from God with a grateful heart.

The third lesson that we can learn from the rich man in Luke 12 is to not be prideful. This is another attribute this rich man demonstrated when he reasoned with himself saying what he should do with his goods, since he had no place to store his crops. He said that he would tear down his barns and build larger ones and he would store up all of his grains and his goods. He made eight references to himself. The Bible tells us that when we have pride God will fight us not Satan. *"You younger men, likewise, be subject to your elders; and all of you, clothe yourselves with humility toward one another, for God is opposed to the proud, but gives grace to the humble."* (1 Peter 5:5)

Being able to humble yourself is not something that requires having a massive prayer meeting about pride. Pride occurs when a person decides to live independent of God. We do not need to pray about humility. We simply need to submit our lives to the will of God (Philippians 2:1-11). If we obey His greatest commandment then we are able to live in the will of God. *"You shall love the Lord your God with all your heart, and with all your soul, and with all your mind. This is the great and foremost commandment."* (Matt 22:37-40; NASU)

Humility is saying 'God your word is true and it is right and although it may not fit with what I think, because you are holy and righteous, I will submit and do whatever you say.' When being a treasurer seeker drives us to depend on our strength, like this rich man, the same God who blesses us humbles us. We do not control own destinies, so we should not lean to our own understanding. We must trust God's purposes by surrendering our will to His will. (Proverbs 3:3-5; 24:3-5)

Material possessions could be here today and gone tomorrow. God is the one that supplies us with all things richly to enjoy. Treasure keepers, unlike treasure seekers, are not eager to keep their money, but they are willing to share their money because they know that God can continually bless them. Their focus is to store up treasures in heaven and not hoard them on earth. *"Give, and it will be given to you; good measure, press down, shaken together, running over, they will pour into your lap. For by your standard of measure it will be measured to you in return."* (Luke 6:38)

This is why God's work prospers when His people prosper. The reason why God blesses us, is so that His work continues for His glory and our continual blessing. He has us here to be blessed so that His work can be blessed. In Proverbs 11:24-26 it says, *"There is one who scatters (who gives, who does good works, who helps to ensure that things are operating) yet increases all the more and there is one who withholds what is justly due. and yet it results only in want. The generous man will be prosperous, and he who waters will himself be watered. He who withholds grain, the people will curse him, but blessing will be on the head of him who sells it." (NASU)* The generous man will be prosperous and he who waters will himself be watered. In other words the person who sows to God kingdom work, God in turn sows to supply their needs on earth.

It is better to be a treasure keeper, instead of a treasure seeker, because the treasure is from God. The rich man in Luke 12 stored up his goods to make his own life comfortable and it became no good to him even when he faced God. He lived rich on earth, but very poor after he died. (Luke 12:21). Hoarding God's blessing is sinful and destructive to those whom God blesses.

We should not seek treasures on this earth, because this is not our eternal home (Colossians 3:1-4). Consider an individual who is making a temporary stop. A man who has a layover at an airport does not go into the bathroom, frown at its décor, and start redecorating!

Why, because he does not live there. He has a home in another place. While he is away, he will get by with only what he absolutely needs, so that he will have more money to furnish his permanent home. So why do we Christians work hard at trying to make our life in this world more comfortable? This is just the airport and we are in transit. (2 Corinthians 5:6-10) We should spend our energy on enhancing our eternal reward, and not worry so much about the bare walls in the airport restrooms." (Illustrations for Biblical Preaching, p.184 #638)

When we are treasure seekers, we are never satisfied because we never have enough. The treasure keepers, on the other hand, have contentment and thus they are satisfied. Unfortunately, treasure seekers never have enough, and they struggle to manage what God has provided. This is why Proverbs 16:8 states: *"Better is a little with righteousness than great income with injustice."*

Ultimately, we must learn to focus on a relationship with God that builds contentment, and then the blessings will come. The Bible is telling us that if we are treasure seekers, then we will have struggles, and we will not be treasure keepers (Luke 8:14; James 4:1-4). A false since of security will also make us think that we have control of our destiny. The fact is it is God who is in control. Thus, it is essential that we seek God and trust Him to faithfully provide for all of our needs (Luke 12:31). This is want makes us treasure keepers because He promises *"gladly to give you the kingdom."* (Luke 12:32)

If we store up riches for ourselves, and are not rich toward God, we end up spiritually poor, and our possessions are worthless. If instead we seek God first, we end up spiritually rich. We may or may not also be materially rich, but God will make sure that our physical needs are met. (Luke 12:31; John 15:5) Once these needs are met, we should learn to be content. Learning to live a life of contentment and trusting in God is what makes treasure keepers, rather than treasure seekers.

C H A P T E R 5

God's Formula for Success

Gold is one of the world's most prized and precious metals. We tend to typically only see gold when it is sparkling in its final state. However, in the initial state, gold does not appear to be such a precious metal. Gold must be refined through a fiery process before it is viewed as valuable. The gold refiner, scoops up a pan full of debris consisting of rocks, dirt, and sticks, in hopes that concealed within the debris is some gold. He adds water to the pan, and then puts the pan over a fire. The heat causes the heavy gold to sink to the bottom, and the debris to float to the top. The refiner then skims off the debris, discards it, and then he puts the mixture over the fire. Again, the gold sinks to the bottom, the debris floats to the top; he removes and discards the debris.

This process is repeated as many times as is necessary until there is no more debris. The goldsmith must keep his eyes on the pan at all times, being careful not to expose the gold to the heat for a moment too long. When all that is left is gold, then the refiner recognizes it and removes it from the heat. Amazingly, he knows that it is gold when he can see his own image in the gold!

God, in His infinite wisdom, is trying to refine us like gold in fire (1 Peter 1:7; 4:12-13). He, too, is careful not to leave us in the fire too long. Christ promises to never give us more than we can bear (1 Corinthians 10:13). However, he may allow us to go through a fiery process until all of our debris has been removed, and we are able to shine like gold. Just like the goldsmith, He knows that we have been refined when He can see His image in us. (1 Corinthians 3:18) It is a fiery process that includes one issue after another, in order to teach us, guide us and mature us. He is trying to teach us that success is based on a process.

Satan, on the other hand, is not interested in a growth process. In fact, Satan knows that if we grow spiritually, then he cannot influence us to sin and become distant from God. This is why God would rather us experience His formula for success. God's formula for success is a process that allows us to gain spiritual maturity through trials and tribulation, on our road to success. God does not grant us success through quick fixes. So then when we encounter trials, we can go back to His process and find ourselves back on track.

One of the primary areas that we may experience trials in life is the area of our finances. Although we may experience financial trials, God will grant us success if we endure His process.

God has all that we need or desire. So the question is, how do we gain access to all that He has for each of us? God's formula for success is based on three major steps.

The first step that we must take is to meet our struggles head on (James 1:2-4). In 1 Samuel 17, David's approach with Goliath provides a great example of how to meet our struggles head on. God allowed Goliath to be perfectly healthy, with no physical or mental ailments when he attempted to fight David. Although Goliath was a feared giant, God allowed David to challenge Goliath.

David went through the process of defeating a lion and a bear so that he could look back and say, if I endured a lion and a bear, then Goliath is nothing to me. He understood the process so he could face his issue with no problem. The truth is, when we want to gain success God's way, He does not remove our struggles, because this is how He trains us (Deut. 8:3-4). We have to make the choice to face our struggles head on, and take the necessary steps to improve any adverse situations.

Secondly, we must be strong in the midst of our trials. God tells us throughout the Bible that if we commit ourselves to His kingdom work, He will not desert us (Matthew 28:20). Philippians 4:13 tells us that we can do all things through Christ who strengthens us. God is saying that we should become so convinced of what being strong means that we believe in our hearts that He will be with us.

Joshua was truly a person who had to find strength in the Lord during the midst of His trials. He lost his best friend, Moses, who he walked with for forty years. All of his fighting men were old and he had to re-train his entire army, which consists of the younger generation. They had been walking in the wilderness for forty years burying their family members. The giants in the promise land have not become midgets. The cities are still fortified and Joshua does not even have a chariot.

Why would God tell him to be strong? God is telling him that success is coming, and he must go forth as God commands. We are not looking at a time when the River Jordan is at low tide and they can easily walk over to the other side. God chooses to send Joshua when the River Jordan is at flood stage. God tells Joshua to go and says nothing about a boat. You would think that when Joshua gets there he would be like Moses with a rod. Joshua experienced trials, but he found his strength in God and he eventually achieved success by making it to the Promised Land. Although trials will come our way, we must also find our strength in God in order for us to experience success.

Thirdly, in our quest for success, we must be courageous. "Only be strong and very courageous..." (Joshua 1:7a) Success does not only mean making a lot of money. Success is achieved when a person creates a plan and is courageous enough to complete the plan despite unexpected obstacles. Courageous people do not let fear guide their decisions. In fact, we all have some type of fear in us. God is not saying that we should never fear, because it was God who said that fear is the beginning of wisdom (Proverbs 9:10). He is saying that we should never have so much fear that we do not have faith to do the things that He has given us the ability, strength and will to do. We have to realize that fear and faith do not mix, just like oil and water does not mix. Fear causes us to feel as though our goals cannot be accomplished because we do not have the resources or the ability to immediately reach our goals. It easy to say that we are believers, but when we allow our fears to guide our actions, then we are not being courageous.

Due to fear, there are some pastors who want to have buildings that are fully paid. They realize that a member could decide to leave at any time. Although, the members could leave at any time, the pastor is committed to staying at the church. Therefore, no one has as much to lose as the pastor. This gives him a greater reason to fear. However, the pastor of a church should not concern himself with the amount of church resources. Rather, the pastor should concern himself with whether or not the church fits into God's vision. Once the church fits within the confines of God's word, then the pastor and the church body can move forward courageously knowing that God will take care of His people.

There are some people who have dreams of reaching a particular career goal. Sometimes these goals are sacrificed because of the fear that the study demands in school cannot be met. There may also be a fear that we may not have enough money to go to college or trade school. However, if we set career goals, we must have the courage, through God's strength, to overcome the obstacles that we may encounter on our roads to success.

When we make decisions in our lives, they must be biblically-based decisions that will lead to success. Making decisions according to God's laws is similar to playing on a basketball court. When basketball players are making decisions on the court, they must not go out of bounds and they must play by a set of rules. Much like the rules for the players in a basketball game, the Lord gives us specific rules to abide by. The Lord tells us to give to Him. However, many of us are waiting to hear from Him as to what we should give. God has already told us what to give, but some believers do not want to be courageous, and they let fear make them hold on to their money.

In Malachi 3:10, God tells us *"Bring the whole tithe into the storehouse, that there may be food in my house. Test me in this, says the Lord Almighty, and see if I will not throw open the floodgates of heaven and pour out so much blessing that you will not have room enough for it.*" We must first trust God with our money by paying our tithes. It does not matter what financial state we are in currently. God knows our situation. Therefore, we must believe in His promise to open the floodgates and pour us out a blessing, when we are faithful in tithing.

Success comes when we are willing to obey whatever God says. God is saying "I understand how we can tremble when we are giving away money that we need, but He says just obey because He commanded it." He says even if we find ourselves panicking, we can go back to the commands that He has given us, because He has promised in His word to take care of us. *"...Teaching them to observe all that I commanded you; and lo, I am with you always, even to the end of the age.*" (Matt 28:20; NASU)

Notice that in the observation of His commands that He is more powerfully supporting us and fighting for us (Romans 8:31). Abraham and Sarah also experienced God's process. God tells Abraham that he is going to be the father of a great nation. Based on this promise, one would think that the Abraham would have triplets or maybe even eight babies at one time. This promise seemed to make no sense at all since they were having their first child when Sarah was seventy-five years old and Abraham was one hundred years old. To make it more confusing, God only gives them one child and later instructs Abraham to sacrifice his son. However, God used their one child, Isaac, because of Abraham's faith, to fulfill His promise of making Abraham the father of a great nation. Success was not achieved because Abraham took Hagar to be a surrogate parent. Matter of fact, these steps create confusion rather than success. Abrahams success was achieved because God was faithful to His promises (Genesis 12:1-3). And by God's grace and Abraham's submission to God's will, Abraham experienced God working for Him (Romans 4:18-21).

One day I was flying in the front part of the plane and noticed that the cockpit door had been left open. I became nosy and decided to see what it was like for a pilot. It was night time and the runway appeared as pretty as it does in the movies. It occurred to me that it was dark, with no street signs, and the pilot was flying through the clouds. The pilot seemed to be flying blindly. So there I was sitting with a little black seat belt around me, as if that would make a difference if the plane went down at 500 miles per hour.

I realized that the only reason that the pilot was able to fly the plane is that he believed in the instrument panel. If the instrument panel said we were upside down, then he would turn the plane back to the proper position. If it said we were going north, when we were supposed to go south, then he would turn the plane around and start heading south. Whatever the instrument panel said is what mattered, because he did not need to see through the windshield until he got ready to land, since he was flying blind. Whatever the maps says is what the navigator follows. He arrived at the airport and I looked over at a plane landing on the other runway. I thanked God for the tower, because in the tower, they see everything. The workers in the tower could tell the pilot, runway 254, and no one else will land on it until it is empty. If it were not for guidance from the tower, pilots would be landing and taking off all at the same time.

Similar to a pilot flying a plane, everyday we also live blind, because we never know what is going to happen from one minute to the next. Although we have a plan, we do not have a clue about what to expect. However, God is telling us to follow the instrument panel (God's Word illuminate by the Holy Spirit). We must forget the storm in front of us and the clouds around us and follow the map. There are times when we have to consult the tower and pray to ask God for direction that we need. We need God's instrument panel every day, in order to discover the success that God has for us. Therefore, we should relax and enjoy the ride that God can create through the power of the Holy Spirit. I guarantee that God's formula will lead to success, because it is guaranteed by God (Joshua 1:5-9; Isaiah 40:28-31; Romans 8: 28-39; Philippians 4:13). God does not lie (Titus 1:2).

"No man will be able to stand before you all the days of your life. Just as I have been with Moses, I will be with you; I will not fail you or forsake you. Be strong and courageous, for you shall give this people possession of the land which I swore to their fathers to give them. Only be strong and very courageous; be careful to do according to all the law which Moses My servant commanded you; do not turn from it to the right or to the left, so that you may have success wherever you go. This book of the law shall not depart from your mouth, but you shall meditate on it day and night, so that you may be careful to do according to all that is written in it; for then you will make your way prosperous, and then you will have success. Have I not commanded you? Be strong and courageous! Do not tremble or be dismayed, for the Lord your God is with you wherever you go." (Joshua 1:5-9; NASU)

This chapter is crucial for the principles shared in this book to become productive for your family. *"Unless the Lord builds the house, they labor in vain who build it; unless the Lord guards the city, the watchman keeps awake in vain. It is vain for you to rise up early, to retire late, to eat the bread of painful labors; For He gives to His beloved even in his sleep."* (Psalm 127:1-2; NASU) *"How blessed is everyone who fears the Lord, who walks in His ways. When you shall eat of the fruit of your hands, you will be happy and it will be well with you. Your wife shall be like a fruitful vine. Within your house, your children like olive plants around your table. Behold, for thus shall the man be blessed who fears the Lord."* (Psalm 128:1-4; NASU)

C H A P T E R **6**

God and Money – 1 Timothy

"You are to be more envied than anyone I know," said a young man to a millionaire. "Why so?" responded the millionaire. "I am not aware of any cause for which I should be envied." "What, sir!" exclaimed the young man. "Why, you are a millionaire! Think of the thousands your income brings every month!" "Well, what of that?" replied the millionaire. "All I get out of it is my food and clothes, and I can't eat more than one man's allowance and wear more than one suit of clothes at a time. Even you can do as much as I can, can't you?" "Yes, but think of the hundreds of fine houses you own, and the rentals they bring you." "What good does that do me?" replied the rich man. "I can only live in one house at a time. As for the money I receive for rents, why, I can't eat or wear it; I can only use it to buy other houses for other people to live in; they are the beneficiaries, not I." Then, finally, after a little more discussion, the millionaire turned to the young man and said: "I can tell you that the less you desire in this life, the happier you will be. All my wealth can't buy a single day more of life, cannot buy back my youth, cannot procure power to keep off the hour of death. Then what will happen? In a few short years, at most, I must lie down in the grave and leave it all forever. Young man, you have no cause to envy me." (Illustrations of Bible Truths, 1998)

Money is powerful in this world, and it can buy a lot of things. Money, however, cannot buy what the fruit of the Spirit produces (Galatians 5:22-26). Money cannot buy joy, peace, love, strength, kindness or gentleness. Because "the love of money is the root of all evil" (1 Timothy 6:10), and Paul wants Timothy to "pursue righteousness, godliness, faith, love, perseverance and gentleness" (1 Timothy 6:11), he instructs Timothy on how to develop a healthy view of money.

There is no better person to teach this than Paul. This is because Paul had *"learned contentment in whatever circumstances I am"* (Philippians 4:11). Paul is also the most qualified to teach about money because at one time Paul did well, but at the end of his ministry Paul was in poverty (Philippians 4:12). He counted all the things he had achieved in life as lost for the sake of serving his calling. Paul learned *"to get along with humble means…"* (Philippians 4:12) as he faithfully served the Lord. Paul did not complain about his circumstances and he also did not allow his circumstances to limit what he faithfully did for Christ.

It is from the lessons Paul sought to teach Timothy that we can learn what God thinks about money. We can learn how to protect ourselves from the corruption that the desire for money can create. In 1 Timothy 6:10, Paul teaches us, *"For the love of money is the root of all kinds of evil. Some people, eager for money, have wandered from the faith and pierced themselves with many griefs."* So what does Paul mean when he refers to the love of money?

The word love, in our culture, can have many meanings. But love in the Bible has more to do with the willful direction a person takes in an effort to fulfill a desire that is important to that individual. When people are in love, they are so committed that they do whatever is necessary to fulfill their desires. Love is an act that is persistent (John 3:16; 14:15). So the first lesson Paul sought to teach Timothy is to not love money (1 Timothy 6:10) that to love money is to be controlled by it.

If every decision an individual makes is controlled by a desire to make money and to get rich, then this individual is in love with money. If believers are consistently covetous, then they are in love with things (Covet - "to stretch one's self out in order to touch or grasp something, to reach after or desire something."). John says to us; *"For all that is in the world, the lust of the flesh and the lust of the eyes and the boastful pride of life, is not from the Father, but is from the world. The world is passing away, and its lusts; but the one who does the will of God lives forever."* (1 John 2:16) In 1 John 5:19, John states, *"We know that we are of God, and that the whole world lies in the power of the evil one."* If most of the decisions made are to make money and to acquire things, then the very focus of every working day is eventually controlled by worldly views, rather than Godly views.

Any one who loves in this manner, does not love God. *"No one can serve two masters; for either he will hate the one and love the other, or he will be devoted to one and despise the other. You cannot serve God and wealth.* (Matt 6:24; NASU) This is why the love of money is the beginning (root) or source of `all of evil.'` (1 Timothy 6:10)

Satan would love for us to be controlled by a desire to make money, and a desire to chase the things of the world. Our desire, James says, is not something that Satan starts; *"Let no one say when he is tempted, "I am being tempted by God"; for God cannot be tempted by evil, and He Himself does not tempt anyone. <u>But each one is tempted when he is carried away and enticed by his own lust.</u>"* (James 1:13-14; NASU) This is why being driven everyday by the desire to get rich leads to sin. This type of desire becomes influenced by the negative purposes of Satan. Many people who are striving to get rich, begin to neglect church, Bible Study, and a substantive prayer life. Often times they even give up spending significant time with their family, in their efforts to get rich.

"Once there were rich parents who left their children constantly in the care of servants. But, like the flower of the grass, riches passed by. The parents could not afford servants which necessitated their taking care of the children. One evening when the father had returned home after a busy and frustrating day at work, his little girl climbed upon his knee and twining her arms around his neck said: 'Daddy, don't get rich again. You did not come into the nursery when you were rich, but now we can be with you and get on your knee and kiss you. Don't get rich again, Daddy. I love you and mommy being here'" (Illustrations of Bible Truths, 1998)

To desire to get rich (1 Timothy 6:10) means to be consumed with achieving what is more than the normal amount of resources necessary to sustain a family. Believers should work with this principle guiding them: *"For we have brought nothing into the world, so we cannot take anything out of it either. If we have good and covering, with these we shall be content. But those who want to get rich fall into temptation and a snare and many foolish and harmful desires which plunge men into ruin and destruction."* (1 Timothy 6:7-9)

Some people's snare is gambling. Some people's snare is relentless shopping. For other individuals, the snare may be working excessively and as a result, neglecting of their families. For others, the snare may be not availing their time to serve God. There are even some individuals whose snare is worshipping God in order to maintain the quality of life they desire. The believers in the Laodicea church did this. *"Because you say, "I am rich, and have become wealthy, and have need of nothing," and you do not know that you are wretched and miserable and poor and blind and naked. I advise you to buy from Me gold refined by fire so that you may become rich, and white garments so that you may clothe yourself, and that the shame of your nakedness will not be revealed; and eye salve to anoint your eyes so that you may see."* (Rev 3:17,18; NASU)

A believer can become blind (2 Peter 1:3-5, 9; Hebrews 5:11-14; Matthew 13:10-17; heard the truth, but did not practice the truth) or deaf when they neglect obeying God, and neglect spiritual growth. This leads to greater possibilities of being influenced by Satan (Acts 5:1-11; Ananias and Sapphira). This is why when believers function this way *`they wander away from the faith.'* It is important for each believer to *"Be of sober spirit, be on the alert. Your adversary, the devil, prowls around like a roaring lion, seeking someone to devour."* (1 Peter 5:8; NASU)

Ananias and Sapphira were devoured by Satan because their desires lead them to sin. The payment for sin can be physical death (Romans 6:23; 1Corinthians 11:28-32; 1 John 5:16). Even Solomon allowed his riches still lead him to ruin.

The Northern Kingdom soon turned to worship gods that Solomon allowed his foreign wives to worship. A nation was destroyed and became very wicked to the point of killing God's prophets. Jezebel was so wicked that she caused a great man of faith Elijah to run and hide (1 Kings 17-19).

After God gave riches to Solomon, instead of using his wisdom to live rich and wise, Solomon sought to acquire all he could of all the world's goods (Ecclesiastes 2:1-11). He became obsessed with the things of the world. His desires became an accumulation of willful acts to achieve things for the sake of satisfying his passions. *"All that my eyes desired I did not refuse them. I did not withhold my heart from any pleasure, for my heart was pleased because of all my labor and this was my reward for all my labor. Thus I considered all my activities which my hands had done and the labor which I had exerted, and behold all was vanity and striving after wind and there was no profit under the sun."* (Ecclesiastes 2:10-11; NASU)

After spending his life seeking all he could, Solomon realized that all this was vanity and vexation of spirit (Ecclesiastes 5:17). These desires corrupted him and ruined a nation. *"I know that there is nothing better for them than to rejoice and to do good in one's lifetime; moreover, that every man who eats and drinks sees good in all his labor — it is the gift of God. I know that everything God does will remain forever; there is nothing to add to it and there is nothing to take from it, for God has so worked that men should fear Him. That which is has been already and that which will be has already been, for God seeks what has passed by."* (Ecclesiastes 3:12-15; NASU)

"This desire to be wealthy is not a passing emotional thing, but the result of a process of reasoning. Mature consideration has been given the matter of the acquisition of riches, with the result that that desire has become a settled and planned procedure. Vincent says: "It is not the *possession* of riches, but the love of them that leads men into temptation." Expositors comments: "The warning applies to all grades of wealth: all come under it whose ambition is to have more money than that which satisfies their accustomed needs. We are also to note that what is here condemned is not an ambition to excel in some lawful department of human activity, which though it bring an increase in riches, develops character, but the having a single eye to the accumulation of money by any means." (Wuest, 1997 1 Ti 6:6)

When money controls an individual's life, then Satan has the ability to influence that person. This can be the beginning of `all sorts of evil'. Evil here means something that can be harmful. The love of money can make a person do whatever it takes to gain more money. The love of money negatively affects the character of individuals, and that love causes them to be `*pierced with many of grief*' (this means complete loss; the destruction of their well being). God wants us to have a healthy view of money so that it works for our benefit, rather than our destruction. "A London newspaper offered a prize for the best definition of money. It was awarded to a young man whose definition was, "Money is an article which may be used as a universal passport to everywhere except heaven and as a universal provider of everything except happiness." (Illustrations of Bible Truths, 1998)

"In our constant struggle to acquire things for the preservation of life we wear out life itself. Wise is he who said: "Worldly riches are like nuts: many clothes are torn in getting them, many a tooth broken in cracking them, and never a belly filled with eating them." Jesus gives us very excellent advice which we shall do well to heed, "Don't wear yourselves out for things which perish so easily." (Illustrations of Bible Truths, 1998)

In 1 Timothy 6:17, Paul instructs Timothy to teach those who are blessed to think in this manner; "*Instruct those who are rich in this present world not to be conceited or to fix their hope on the uncertainty of riches, but on God, who richly supplies us with all things to enjoy. Instruct them to do good, to be rich in good works, to be generous and ready to share, storing up for themselves the treasure of a good foundation for the future, so that they may take hold of that which is life indeed.*" (NASU)

Timothy is instructed to give the church's rich members direction in the same manner a military leads their troops. They are ordered to not hoard money or spend their life seeking after riches. They must not become conceited. Conceited means to become proud and lifted up because of money. There is of no certainty that life continues and that man can find enjoyment from having money. Christ explained in the parable about the rich man in Matthew 6:13-21 (We discussed this earlier in this book).

It is God who provides wealth; *"But you shall remember the LORD your God, for it is He who is giving you power to make wealth that He may confirm His covenant which He swore to your fathers, as it is this day. It shall come about if you ever forget the LORD your God and go after other gods and serve them and worship them, I testify against you today that you will surely perish. Like the nations that the LORD makes to perish before you, so you shall perish; because you would not listen to the voice of the LORD your God.* (Deut. 8:18; NASU). This is why God views believers as His stewards, rather than producers of wealth.

Job lost all his possessions and his family in a shorter time than it took him to accumulate his wealth. Just as God gave it to him, God allowed Satan, the destroyer, to take it from him. Job, a righteous man, meaning a man who committed his life to live by the standards and justice of God, recognized God for his blessing and respected his sovereign will. In the midst of his sorrow and loss, Job said, *"The LORD gave and the LORD has taken away. Blessed be the name of the LORD."* (Job 1:21; NASU) Job did not put his trust in his wealth. His trust and direction for life was in the Lord. *"He who trusts in his riches will fall, but the righteous will flourish like the green leaf."* (Prov. 11:28; NASU) Because Job accepted the discipline of God and therefore the love of God, he completely trusted in God not the uncertainty of riches. *He said, 'Naked I came from my mother's womb, and naked I shall return there.* (Job 1:21; NASU) God can supply us with all of our needs according to His riches in glory (Philippians 4:19) God can also bless our wishes if we choose to abide in Him (John 15:5, 7).

When God supplies riches it is enjoyed (1 Timothy 6:17), but when man seeks after riches it leads to his ruin and gives him `*many griefs*.' It is better to have God be the supplier of our wealth, rather than for man to strive all the days of his life and find vanity. So it is better Paul says for the rich to take their wealth and do well. It is for this purpose that we are Christ workmanship (Ephesians 2:10). To do 'good' is to take the resources God supplies and become productive for his kingdom (1 Corinthians 10:31). *"Worthy are You, our Lord and our God, to receive glory and honor and power; for You created all things, and because of Your will they existed, and were created."* (Rev 4:11; NASU)

"We should use our wealth to do good to others; we should share; we should put our money to work. When we do, we enrich ourselves spiritually, and we make investments for the future." (Luke 16:1–13). *"That they may lay hold on eternal life"* (1 Timothy 6:19) does not suggest that these people are not saved. *"That they may lay hold on the life that is real"* would express it perfectly. Riches can lure a person into a make-believe world of shallow pleasure. But riches *plus God's will* introduce a person to life that is real and ministry that is lasting.

When we commit to do 'good,' it is a result of the workmanship that Christ is doing in us through the Holy Spirit (Ephesians 2:10; 3:15-17). So the more we focus on obeying Him, under the direction of the Holy Spirit, is the more we experience His imputed righteousness. This is experiencing the benefits of eternal life. Remember; *"the effective fervent prayer of the righteous avails much."* (James 5:16) Also, the righteous never goes begging bread. This is why the real issue is committing to live righteous rather than trying, on our own, to grain much. *"He who trusts in his riches will fall, but the righteous will flourish like the green leaf."* (Proverbs 11:28; NASU) *"The wages of the righteous is life, the income of the wicked, punishment."* (Proverbs 10:16)

In actuality, God does want us to enjoy the wealth he has provided. *"Furthermore, as for every man to whom God has given riches and wealth, He has also empowered him to eat form them and to receive his reward and rejoice in his labor; this is the gift of God."* (Ecclesiastes. 5:19) In fact, one of the recurring themes in Ecclesiastes is, *"Enjoy the blessings of life now, because life will end one day"* (Ecclesiastes. 2:24; 3:12–15, 22; 5:18–20; 9:7–10; 11:9–10). This is not sinful 'hedonism,' living for the pleasures of life. It is simply enjoying all that God gives us for His glory. *"There is nothing better for a man than to eat and drink and tell himself that his labor is good. This also I have seen that it is from the hand of God."* (Ecclesiastes 2:24-25; NASU)

A proper attitude towards money allows believers to experience joy, rather than trouble. *"It is the blessing of the Lord that makes rich, and He adds no sorrow to it."* (Proverbs 10:22) Joy is the result of walking with God. A believer's walk with God produces life, and life more abundantly (John 10:10). This walk with God also develops the fruits of the Spirit (Galatians 5:22-25).

So not only do believers have their riches to enjoy, but their riches bless others' enjoyment. Every time believers give, God gives back to them (Luke 6:38) more than they can distribute. *"Furthermore, as for every man <u>to whom God has given riches and wealth</u>, He has also empowered him to eat from them and to receive his reward and rejoice in his labor; this is the gift of God. For he will not often consider the years of his life,* *because God keeps him occupied with the gladness of his heart."* (Ecclesiastes 5:19-20: NASU)

"Henry P. Crowell, affectionately called "The autocrat of the Breakfast Table," contracted tuberculosis when a boy and couldn't go to school. After hearing a sermon by Dwight L. Moody, young Crowell prayed, "I can't be a preacher, but I can be a good businessman. God, if You will let me make money, I will use it in Your service." (Tan, *Encyclopedia of 7700 illustrations, 1996)*

"Under the doctor's advice, Crowell worked outdoors for seven years and regained his health. He then bought the little run-down Quaker Mill at Ravanna, Ohio. Within ten years, Quaker Oats was a household word to millions. Crowell also operated the huge Perfection Stove Company. For over 40 years, Henry P. Crowell faithfully gave 60 to 70 percent of his income to God's causes, having advanced from an initial 10%." (Tan, *Encyclopedia of 7700 illustrations, 1996)* God took a poor ill man and made him healthy and wealthy only for this wealthy, healthy man to bless God kingdom with God's resources. Like Job, he never forgot where his blessings came from. This man's product now blesses people long after his death.

C H A P T E R 7

It's Not All About Money

Some people who read this book may think that I am saying it is better to be poor; we should exploit God's Word to get rich or just be happy to remain in our state. This is so far from the truth even a space ship could not find it. If you believe this, then you have misunderstood the purpose of this book.

My focus is we must love God so that every desire is to experience Him, trust Him and glorify Him. It is to extend the relationship of the Trinity that God created man. *"Then God said, "Let Us make man in Our image, according to Our likeness; and let them rule over the fish of the sea and over the birds of the sky and over the cattle and over all the earth, and over every creeping thing that creeps on the earth." God created man in His own image, in the image of God He created him; male and female He created them. God blessed them; and God said to them, "Be fruitful and multiply, and fill the earth, and subdue it; and rule over the fish of the sea and over the birds of the sky and over every living thing that moves on the earth."* (Gen 1:26-29; NASU)

Love by its very nature is to share itself (1 John 3:16-19). Married couples who love each other dearly, desire to have children. God, Christ and the Holy Spirit by their very nature is love (1 John 4:16). This love extends itself to man to create a loving relationship (John 3:16; 1 John 4:9). Man's sinful acts separated God from man. Christ death provided forgiveness for our sins so that once we accept Him, we are reconciled to God (Colossians 1:15-18).

Once saved, the greater the spiritual development the greater the fellowship and the better the relationship. *"For all who are being led by the Spirit of God, these are sons of God."* (Romans 8:14) *"Greater love has no one than this, that on lay down his life for his friends."* (John 15:13) As a result, believers should be able to say, like Paul; *"I have been crucified with Christ; and it is no longer I who live, but Christ lives in me; and the life which I now live in the flesh I live by faith in the Son of God, who loved me and gave Himself up for me."* (Gal 2:20-21; NASU) It is from the relationship that God establishes that man is blessed.

When God made Adam and Eve, He placed them in a garden fully prepared for their enjoyment. Adam had so much work (Genesis 1:28-31; 2:15) to do that God said he needed a helper, not just a wife. God waited until He made man and then created a need for man to work. It was always God's divine purpose that man is blessed from his labor. *"Now no shrub of the field was yet in the earth, and no plant of the field had yet sprouted, for the LORD God had not sent rain upon the earth, and there was no man to cultivate the ground. But a mist used to rise from the earth and water the whole surface of the ground. Then the LORD God formed man of dust from the ground, and breathed into his nostrils the breath of life; and man became a living being."* (Gen 2:5-8; NASU)

Adam could not multiply and fill the earth by himself and at the same time work. He needed a helper. God did all of this for Adam and Eve, but always made a point to come and fellowship with them. (Genesis 3:8) Everything Adam and Eve did was directed by God. Every purpose that Adam and Eve served was directed by God. God was not only their creator, He was the God whom their worshipped. They lived blessed (in His creative order He said He would bless them) not needing anything, so there was no need for them to eat from `the tree of good and evil.'

It is from a person's labor they are blessed. This is why God speaks out against laziness (Proverbs 6:6-11), and refuses to feed a person who does not work. (2 Thessalonians 3:10). God is not seeking to punish the person; He is seeking to direct them to experience the blessing of tilling His garden focused on His purposes. This is because *"the hand of the diligent will rule, but the slack hand will be put to forced labor."* (Proverbs

13:24) Not only do the diligent rule, their work makes them rich. *"Poor is he who works with a negligent hand, but the hand of the diligent makes rich."* (Proverbs 10:4)

A person can go to their job and work hard, not to the neglect of their family, and trust God to promote them. When the work is done, in obedience to God's Word, the person is rewarded by God. The Bible teaches that God rewards faith (Hebrews 11:6) and faith is obedience to the Word of God without having to see the results before we obey. We obey God based on how faithful He has been in the past, because this is the evidence of His power that we trust (Hebrews 11:1).

When a person works, it is in obedience to Colossians 3:23-24; *"Whatever you do, do your work heartily, as for the Lord rather than for me, knowing that form the Lord you will receive the reward of the inheritance. It is the Lord Christ whom you serve."* As a result; *"What ever your hand finds to do, do it with all your might; for there is no activity or planning or knowledge or wisdom in Sheol where you are going."* (Ecclesiastes 9:10) Therefore, it is not just going to work, it is working diligently not for the boss (we are not eye servants; Ephesians 6:5-9), but always for the Lord and His purposes.

The minute Satan tempted Eve and she become more controlled by the desire for the garden than the direction of the Gardener and when Adam followed sin led mankind to ruin and destruction. *"Then the woman saw that the tree was good for food, and that it was a delight to the eyes, and that the tree was desirable to make one wise, she took from its fruit and ate; and she gave also to her husband with her, and he ate."* (Gen 3:6-7; NASU)

Fulfilling the commands of God (Genesis 1:27-31; 2:15) became more of a burden than a joy. Eve followed her desire and how delightful the tree was to her eyes. Satan continues to cause things to be delightful to the eyes so that the flesh, that is now weak, will desire it. It is our desire, says James, and the lust of the flesh that leads to sin and destruction (James 1:13-15; 1 John 2:15-17).

When believers obey these passions and allow themselves to be controlled by it, then they prove they love material wealth more than God. Once this occurs, God says it becomes their god (Matthew 6:24). This is why chasing get rich schemes are not profitable for a believer. *"He who tills his land will have plenty of bread, but he who pursues worthless things lacks sense. He who tills his land will have plenty of food, but he who follows empty pursuits will have poverty in plenty."* (Proverbs 12:11; Prov 28:19; NASU) This is because they follow the lust of the flesh and what is pleasing to the eyes rather to trust God and obey Him which means they work with their hands.

"It is the blessing of the Lord that makes rich, and He adds no sorrow to it." (Proverbs 10:22) Yes, the verse does say rich. We can strive for it based on our desires or we can trust God based on His Word. *"By wisdom a house is built, and by understanding it is established; and by knowledge the rooms are filled with all precious and pleasant riches."* (Proverbs 24:3-4; 3:16) Notice again he says riches. God has no problem with blessing His people just like He did Solomon, but it is not so they become obsess with 'the garden' rather than the Gardener.

Does this mean that everyone becomes rich? Christ clearly stated that the poor will always be in the world. (John 12:8) Christ responds this way, because if the poor lived righteously, they never beg for bread. If the poor lived righteously, He establishes them in their ways. If the poor fear God, He causes their children to become like olive plants and bless them with long life (Psalm 128). So even though by world standards, the poor are poor by Biblical standards, they are rich because of God. *"And my God will supply all your needs according to His riches in glory in Christ Jesus."* (Phil 4:19; NASU)

Many African-Americans who grew up in humble means never knew they were poor until they were told by someone. God so blessed them and some had such a rich family life that they did not know they were missing anything. I remember people telling me I grew in a third world country.

That really surprised me, because I did not know that where I grew up was considered a third world country.

Fundamental to everything I have said is for believers to seek God in everything (Luke 12:31-34; Proverbs 10:3, 30; 11:8, 16, 31; 13:20; 24:16) rather than what is delightful to their eyes. *"The wages of the righteous is life (*not just money*), the income of the wicked, punishment."* (Proverbs 11:16; please notice it is not that the wicked don't have income) When believers abide in Christ; life flows in and through them (Colossians 3:1-4). Bearing fruit produces the character (John 15:1-5) of Christ, re-establishes fellowship with God, directs the daily life of a believer and orders their purpose for living (Rev. 4:11). This blesses them to enjoy the Spirit of God and therefore provides inner strength (Ephesians 3:16-17) to deal with the continual struggles of living with the enemy (Satan).

God then blesses believers to experience their desires (John 15:7-8) that are controlled and directed by Him as it was with Adam (Romans 5:12-21). *"But we all, with unveiled face, beholding as in a mirror the glory of the Lord, are being transformed into the same image from glory to glory, just as from the Lord, the Spirit."* (2 Corinthians 3:18; NASU). As a result believers enjoy God as well as enjoy all He wants to bless us with in His garden (His earth) that He sustains (Hebrews 1:3).

"The conclusion, when all has been heard, is: fear God and keep His commandments, because this applies to every person. For God will bring every act to judgment, everything which is hidden, whether it is good or evil." (Ecclesiastes 12:13-14; NASU)

Our Vision

The vision of Power Walk Ministries Inc. is to partner with churches to disciple leaders and others based on biblical training as modeled by Jesus Christ in an effort to impact the community and the world for the glory of God.

Our Mission

Power Walk Ministries' mission is to empower church leaders, families, singles and married couples through biblical training to positively change the home, church, and community for the glory of God. This is accomplished through leadership conferences, church consultations, radio ministries, video training, and the distribution of manuals and books locally, nationally, and internationally.

Our Focus

The focus of Power Walk Ministries is to `change lives one step at a time'. This empowers leaders from the inside out. When leaders are spiritually challenged, their walk with God becomes a powerful influence to others. This in turn affects not just churches, but also homes and communities. Spiritual growth along with training and material causes a leader to be productive for God's glory.

Dr. Paul Cannings' zeal for leaders of the local churches and parishioners is to equip and empower them to be effective in their respective ministries. As Dr. Cannings was led to start Power Walk ministries, he wanted to provide quality training with practical application so that leaders can both assess and address the pressing, spiritual needs of their local churches and communities.

As founder of a church, Dr. Cannings passionately desires to accomplish strength in the body of Christ bearing in mind the guidelines that were biblically developed. In his training tool, "Biblical Answers for the 21st Century Church," Dr. Cannings mentions, "I became involved in writing documents that served as a resource for many churches so that they can resolve issues from a "biblio-centric" perspective." His mandate is that in order to impact the world, it must begin with the leaders in the church. Equipping leaders with the appropriate tools to impact their church body is the heartbeat of Power Walk Ministries.

The Need

Power Walk Ministries exist to assist pastors, by providing material that guides them to stimulate spiritual growth in their leaders. Power Walk Ministries' goal is to meet the pressing needs of local churches, primarily in the urban communities, so that pastors and leaders can effectively minister to the diverse needs of leaders, parishioners and the community. It is designed to train these leaders to be great husbands, fathers, wives or mothers. This also teaches them how to work with their pastor as they seek to minister to the needs of congregants. It is designed to assist the pastor in establishing the Lord's vision in the life of the church and how to effectively expand the vision into the surrounding communities. Pastors and leaders are provided material and training so that they can quickly apply this information to the ongoing development of their churches, which in turn impacts the community to effectively bring about change.

How to Help

Becoming a Partner with Power Walk Ministries will truly be an awarding experience. Your contributions will help us reach and teach leaders in a variety of ways. Your contributions will help us to expand the distribution channels of our current book publications, expand conference dates and locations and to broaden radio and television production capabilities worldwide.

For more information or to donate, please contact:
Mayphous Collins
Power Walk Ministries
7350 TC Jester Blvd.
Houston, Texas 77088
281-260-7402
www.powerwalkministries.org

www.ingramcontent.com/pod-product-compliance
Lightning Source LLC
Chambersburg PA
CBHW071006040426
42443CB00007B/680